"Youth ministry has always been about seeing the lives of students changed by the power of the gospel message. It requires the time-tested, biblical principles Jeff Lovingood has practiced for more than two decades of effective youth ministry. *Make It Last* challenges youth leaders everywhere to get in the game with a strategic plan that will reach students with that message now! You will find Jeff's passion for sharing Christ both contagious and unrelenting. Youth leaders everywhere will be inspired to take the field and go for the biggest win of all: winning students to Christ."

—TROY W. TEMPLE, PhD, associate professor of youth and family ministry, associate dean for master's studies, director of professional doctoral studies, The School of Church Ministries at The Southern Baptist Theological Seminary

"Jeff Lovingood is a great student pastor. His ministry answers the calling of an evangelist while embracing the philosophy of a coach and fulfilling the role of a pastor. Anyone who cares deeply about leading and shepherding students needs this resource."

—BRENT CROWE, vice president, Student Leadership University

"As a revolutionary leader, Jeff has seen unprecedented success by applying the God-given principles that fill this book. Thank you, Jeff, for your willingness to pass them on."

—DAVID NASSER, pastor, Christ City Church, Birmingham, Alabama; author and speaker

"For more than twenty years, Jeff has successfully navigated his way through the labyrinth of church youth ministry. Throughout that time, he has seen new trends, fads, and philosophies come and go. *Make It Last* is a collection of best practices that have proven to produce lasting fruit in students. Jeff shares compelling ideas and principles that have been sifted through his lens of experience and wisdom. If you are looking for challenging and insightful youth ministry coaching from a proven leader, this

—DARREN
Willow Creek Con

D1169473

"When Jeff Lovingood talks about ministry to students, anyone who knows anything about student ministry listens intently. The reason is simple: There is no one in the United States who can speak with the authority, integrity, and experience that Jeff brings to the table when it comes to reaching students with the gospel of Jesus Christ. This book is a rare combination of biblical truth and practical, hands-on ministry wisdom. Get a copy for you and everyone you know who loves teenagers."

— CLAYTON KING, founder and president, Crossroads Ministries; teaching pastor, NewSpring Church, Anderson, South Carolina; campus pastor, Liberty University

"*Make It Last* is a valuable book that provides guidance for building a ministry that produces real and lasting life-change in students and their parents. I have seen firsthand how Jeff has built thriving student ministries at several churches using the principles he shares in this book. He writes from experience as someone who is in the trenches with students every day. If you care about reaching the next generation, this is a must-read!"

— DAVID LANDRITH, senior pastor, Long Hollow Baptist Church, Hendersonville, Tennessee

"When some think of student ministry, they think of lock-ins, fellowships, camps, and activities. Not me. I think of Jeff Lovingood. He is a proven leader among leaders, and he has earned the right to author a book titled *Make It Last* because he has lasted. His principles are proof of how you and the Lord's ministry through you can last as well."

— KEN WHITTEN, senior pastor, Idlewild Baptist Church, Lutz, Florida

"Jeff Lovingood loves the church and has served faithfully over the last twenty-five years. The principles given here are timeless and secure. They are commonly held by pastors who count it a great joy to serve the bride of Christ."

— STEVEN WRIGHT, student pastor and author

MAKE IT LAST

PROVEN PRINCIPLES FOR EFFECTIVE STUDENT MINISTRY

JEFF LOVINGOOD

NAVPRESS

Discipleship Inside Out™

Discipleship Inside Out

NavPress is the publishing ministry of The Navigators, an international Christian organization and leader in personal spiritual development. NavPress is committed to helping people grow spiritually and enjoy lives of meaning and hope through personal and group resources that are biblically rooted, culturally relevant, and highly practical.

For a free catalog go to www.NavPress.com
or call 1.800.366.7788 in the United States or 1.800.839.4769 in Canada.

NavPress titles may be purchased in bulk for ministry, educational, business, fundraising, or sales promotional use. For information, please call NavPress Special Markets at 1.800.504.2924.

ISBN-13: 978-1-61747-834-5

Cover design by Arvid Wallen

Some of the anecdotal illustrations in this book are true to life and are included with the permission of the persons involved. All other illustrations are composites of real situations, and any resemblance to people living or dead is coincidental.

Scripture quotations in this publication are taken from The Holy Bible, English Standard Version (ESV), copyright © 2001 by Crossway Bibles, a division of Good News Publishers. Used by permission. All rights reserved; and the Holy Bible, *Today's New International® Version* (TNIV)®. Copyright © 2001, 2005 by International Bible Society®. Used by permission of International Bible Society. All rights reserved worldwide.

Lovingood, Jeff.
  Make it last : proven principles for effective student ministry / Jeff Lovingood.
     p. cm.
  Includes bibliographical references.
  ISBN 978-1-61747-834-5
  1. Church work with students. I. Title.
  BV4447.L67 2012
  259'.25—dc23
                              2011030753

Printed in the United States of America

1 2 3 4 5 6 7 8 / 17 16 15 14 13 12

To my lovely wife, Rachel, whom I've been married to for the last twenty-three years.

You have supported me in ministry and helped with this book in so many ways.

Also to my kids — Trevor, Kelsey, and Riley — who love their dad no matter what.

CONTENTS

ACKNOWLEDGMENTS

Special thanks to the staff at Long Hollow Baptist Church and especially the pastor, my longtime friend, David Landrith. I'd like to thank Brent Crowe and Jay Strack for encouraging me to write this book. Thanks to all the students, youth workers, and parents I've met in my years of student ministry. To the pastors I've had the privilege of serving under—Lawrence Cox, Danny Wood, O. S. Hawkins, Allen Lockerman, Ken Whitten, and Doug Sager—thank you for giving me the opportunity to work with and learn from you. Gene Mims, you took a chance on a young college student by allowing me to intern on your staff. I will forever be grateful for that and for the encouragement you have continued to supply over all these years. Thanks to Jim Gibson, Rick Jenkins, and Alan Duncan. You each took the time to invest in and challenge me to serve the Lord with a passion for student ministry. Thank you to a loving mom, Jean Ann Lovingood, and to my wife, Rachel, for your support, help, encouragement, and inspiration over the years.

And thank you to Jesus for letting me do what I love best.

FOREWORD

Rumors of the death of student ministry in the local church are greatly exaggerated. Jeff Lovingood and the amazing God-story of Long Hollow Church in Hendersonville, Tennessee, is dispelling those rumors and giving hope to a large tribe of generational leaders.

I recently spoke to a group of Army Senior Chaplains at their annual Strategic Leader Development Training. I presented research to a diverse audience that focused on the thoughts and dreams of the Millennial generation (born 1980–2000). Millennials are now the largest generation in American history (more than eighty million). They are spiritually open yet woefully underexposed to the gospel of Jesus. Life expectancy is currently eighty years old and will continue to rise.

How important is reaching this generation for Christ as early as possible? When a teenager embraces Christ, we influence thousands, if not millions, of people for the gospel over the next sixty to seventy years. We have influenced the friends, family, and communities that will surround that teenager for years to come. Both opportunity and responsibility beg for multiple voices and strategies to rescue this great generation.

Reaching the Millennials for Christ by all means makes this book mission critical. Life-changing student ministry through local churches is one great way to make a difference. I have lived in Nashville since 2007 and witnessed firsthand the God-story of Long Hollow and Jeff Lovingood's ministry. I have one Millennial teen daughter, who lives in my home, and two younger daughters, who will be shaped very much by her and her generation. Because of my love for Christ and my family I have a vested interest in the ministry of the local church for this generation.

One of my favorite movies (remember, I have kids) is *Kung Fu Panda*. The animated film features the voice of Jack Black starring as Po the Panda. Po is trying to discover himself through Kung Fu. The movie has a great line that describes Po's failed quest to find the secret of being a legendary Kung Fu Master. The line in essence is, "The secret is that there is no secret." Po learns that he is responsible for becoming all he was meant to be.

When it comes to "life-changing" youth ministry, Jeff gets it. This book provides no shortcuts or magic bullets to help your youth ministry grow from twenty to eight hundred. The secret is, there is no secret. You will learn that in the following pages. Passion, vision, intentionality, and just plain people skills are keys to making things happen.

What you will find here are incredibly relevant, if not urgent, principles that will help you reach the most lost generation in America's history. Will the principles produce numeric growth such as Long Hollow's? That's unknown. Numeric growth is relative. But will the principles help you create environments for life-changing youth ministry? I say yes. No matter how big your community, whether you are urban, suburban, or rural, that is the clear target, right?

Make It Last. This will be just another book if you choose for it to be. However, let me challenge you to refuse the temptation to waste a great resource. Jeff's passion and experience can offer value to your influence for Christ in your community. At the end of each chapter, you will find a section called "Make It Last." It is a place to make plans as a result of what you read and press toward the goal of reaching this generation for the gospel. So, take your time, get away, read, pray, dream, and write. Then, take action for the glory of God and the souls of the Millennials. Make it last.

Ed Stetzer
president, LifeWay Research

INTRODUCTION

It was a bitterly cold, crisp early-December night in Tennessee. The lights were on. The football field was ready. People crowded into the stands as two teams prepared to take the field and battle for the high school state championship title. In one locker room, players gathered for a pregame chapel. The coach had finished his talk, the team just moments away from taking the field. Stepping in front of the players, I began to call some of the seniors by name. Looking them directly in the eyes, I quietly said to each, "It's time. It's time."

I reflected on the hard work they put into the previous four years, the struggles they overcame, and their passion for the game. As I looked around, I could see it in their eyes. Everyone agreed. It was time to finish what they started, time for them to win the highest prize. They would work together as a team, go for the glory, and do what they had the opportunity to do. They would be state champions.

As the players listened intently, they leaned forward, hands tightening into fists or firmly clutching their helmets. Tension built in the room, and a fierce look of determination crossed their faces. These players were ready. They had prepared for this moment, and the opportunity was upon them.

It was their time.

The Buccaneers went out that night, played an exceptional game, and defeated their opponents, earning the title, "State Champions."

My message for the Buccaneers that night was simple. It is the same message I have for those of you in student ministry today. It's time.

It's time for us as student pastors to take seriously the challenge to reach the world with the message of Jesus Christ, one student at a time. The opportunity is here, and it's time for us to do what we have been called to do in the most effective way possible. It's time for us to build our ministries on proven principles so that lives will continue to be changed for years to come.

I love a pregame speech because it's the last thing a team hears before they face their opponent. A great pregame speech challenges players to take risks, utilizing all they have learned, as they strive to accomplish the goal. This is my pregame speech to you, the leader in student ministry. God wants to use us to make a difference in the lives of those influenced by our ministries. It's a challenge we cannot take lightly; we, like the Buccaneers, must possess fierce determination.

Make It Last will help you understand the purpose God has called us to fulfill as student pastors. As you study the proven principles of each chapter and work through the practical reflection exercises in the "Make It Last" section at the end of each chapter, you'll learn how to develop and paint the picture of your ministry's plan, multiply yourself, and celebrate the life-change God will bring about through your ministry. Are you ready to develop a student ministry whose impact lasts longer than you do? The challenge is before you.

The victory is waiting.

It's time.

CHAPTER 1

START WITH THE INSIDE: HAVE PURPOSE

Have you ever wanted to quit? To just throw in the towel and go get a nine-to-five job? You probably do every Monday or so. There was a time in my ministry life that the pressure on me was very heavy. I felt as if there had to be a certain number of kids getting saved and a certain number of baptisms happening. This pressure began causing all sorts of physical health issues for me, and some days all I could think about was giving up and going home. I regularly asked myself if it was really worth it. I questioned the purpose of my life in ministry and wondered, *Why?*

Reflecting on that question, I considered some of the leaders of the Bible. Can you imagine being Moses and having to deal with all the whining and complaining that the children of Israel subjected him to? It could be comparable to what happens with students on a long bus trip when the air conditioner goes out thirty minutes into the ten-hour drive. What could have possibly kept that man going through all those trials and tribulations? Nothing but God. Moses had been assigned by God to do a task (called to a ministry) and I can just imagine him recalling that burning bush and reminding himself that it really happened. God had spoken to him and called him to lead. Do you think he ever wanted to quit? Of course, and you can read about it in Exodus, but there was a purpose for his life so he kept going. We as pastors need to recognize the plan God has for us so that when people—others on church staff, the congregation, parents, or even students—forget about the purpose of our ministry, we can remind them and encourage them to see the big picture.

This concept is not new. When I was in seminary, I had the opportunity to hear Bob Taylor share about the early years of youth ministry, and the light went on in my head. He talked about how it all started in the early 1970s when youth ministry transitioned from youth directors (people who kept kids busy with activities) to youth ministers. At that time there were some great men of God who saw youth ministry as being about more than babysitting. They saw that God had a purpose for them and for the students they served. It was time to develop a ministry, not just a program. Since understanding this transformation of youth ministry, I've become convinced that knowing God's purpose is vital to its success as a means of creating transformation in the lives of students.

When I have the opportunity to work with youth pastors, I like to ask, "What's your purpose for doing youth ministry? Is it for evangelism, for having a large Wednesday night service, for discipleship, to teach the Bible, to have a strong parent-led ministry?" Of course these are all good things to do and many of them may be a part of a vibrant ministry, but remember, the Bible offers us some insight into what we as ministers and leaders should consider our purpose. Ephesians 4:12 commands us "to equip the saints for the work of ministry, for building up the body of Christ" (ESV). You see, the good things mentioned above are all part of the work of the ministry and are important, but we as the pastors must realize that our main job is to equip the saints (students, parents, and workers) for God's work—building up the body of Christ, helping others grow in their faith and relationship with Christ. Understanding and embracing this God-given purpose will give us the strength to carry on in times when we become discouraged.

Like Moses, when I feel like quitting ministry, I think about that time in my life when God called me. He chose me, Jeff Lovingood, with all my issues, to serve Him and minister in His name, and He chose you, too! When God calls us, He alone should decide when and if we will quit — not us. It's sad to realize that there are pastors across the country who are quitting ministry and giving up on a weekly basis. According to George Barna and The Fuller Institute, more than 1,700 pastors left the ministry each month in 2009. That doesn't include the 1,300 pastors who were terminated by their churches each month.[1] This doesn't have to happen, and there are some principles you can apply to your ministry that will help strengthen you and carry you through the times you are tempted to give up. The most effective tool I have found is to remember God's calling on my life and why I do what I do.

I will never forget when I was a high school senior in Cleveland, Tennessee. Although I was a terrible singer, I was part of the youth choir at First Baptist Church. You might wonder why a person who is tone deaf would be in the choir, and I admit I was part of it for many reasons, several of which were not so spiritual. For instance, a young man could meet many nice Christian girls if he sang in the choir. But that's beside the point. One night, after singing at Ridgecrest in Asheville, North Carolina, we all piled back into the school bus that would take us home. I didn't really feel like talking and was just sitting there doing nothing when the strangest feeling came over me.

It was as if my whole insides were churning. Something was stirring inside me and I didn't really know what that was all about. I wasn't sick; I wasn't upset, but I was definitely feeling something. The longer I sat there thinking about it and trying to decide what was wrong with me, the more it felt like the Lord was trying to get my attention. If you have ever felt God speaking to you inside your heart and mind, then you know what I'm talking about. I started to realize that He must have something that He wanted me to do.

This was quite a shock to me because I couldn't imagine what God could possibly want with me. My experience up to that point was that God's speaking had been mostly about my sin, pointing out my need for repentance and forgiveness. I knew I was saved and had been baptized, and for the most part I felt like I was really doing what God expected me to do. It was really confusing. So when we got back from the choir trip, I met with my youth minister, Jim Gibson, and told him what was happening. I was hoping that he could straighten me out and help me find a little peace.

Jim asked me if I thought God might be calling me to youth ministry. That completely shocked me, to say the least. I had never considered that God could use me. In my mind I felt like I was way too messed up and not smart enough to be a minister. I never did well in school, couldn't read aloud (especially the Bible), and had actually spent two years in seventh grade. Despite all those facts, Jim advised me to pray about it, and for two weeks I prayed. During that time, God continued doing a work in me.

At the end of those two weeks, I finally accepted that with God all things are possible and it was just crazy enough of an idea to be from Him. During a Sunday morning service, I went forward and asked the church to pray for me because I felt the Lord was calling me to ministry. If I was surprised, I figured that other people would be too, but the most amazing thing happened. God used others to confirm His plans for me. He gave me a purpose for my future in the ministry.

A lot has been said about purpose over the last few years and much of it has been very helpful, whether it was about building a vision or constructing an entire ministry. My goal with this chapter is to help you see the role that purpose not only *can* have but *must* have on your life as a pastor or youth leader.

WHY PURPOSE MATTERS

Purpose is more than the title of a movement; it is the central principle for enduring, effective ministry. When you get a grip on your purpose, everything is affected. It's such a huge concept that really has no limit. In organizing the material for this chapter, it became clear to me that the typical linear or sequential kind of outline wouldn't work because the effects of purpose don't flow like that. This is going to take a different kind of thinking to really wrap your brain around it, but if you take the time to understand why purpose matters, you will be well on your way to developing a more effective and enduring student ministry. I like visuals, and I hope you do too. Check this out.

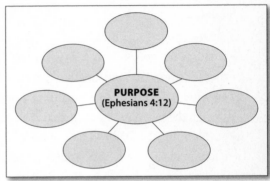

As you take a look at the diagram to the right, you can see that purpose is at the center—and that is where we start— inside of you, the leader. There is really no limit to the number of lines that can be drawn out from purpose just as there is no limit to the ways that purpose can impact your life and ministry. Think about it this way: Purpose is who you are, a servant, called by God, who prepares and equips the saints to also understand their roles as servants in the Kingdom.

CORE VALUES

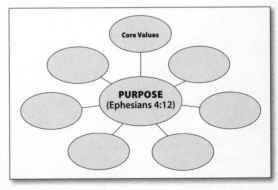

The first principle of student ministry that we're going to look at is "Core Values." Your core values are what you do in your ministry because of who you are. They are the visible manifestations of your God-given purpose. For example, because your purpose is to equip the saints for Kingdom work, one of the core values of your ministry might be that the Scriptures are true and sufficient for addressing all circumstances and areas of life. Another may be to passionately know, love, and become like Jesus. Clearly outlining and daily living out the core values of your ministry will reinforce your commitment to the purpose God has given you as the leader.

Feelings of Insignificance

Even after you've identified your purpose and core values, there may be times when your role as a youth pastor feels like you're just baby-sitting or party planning. You might even feel like your position is not as important as other ministerial roles, but this is far from the truth. Although there is a myth out there that youth ministry is a lesser posi-tion, the reality is that you have been given the privilege to reach a generation for the Lord. When you realize that your purpose, although not as glamorous or visible as others, is just as real and important because of who has called you, the way other people treat you is irrelevant. As I mentioned earlier, your purpose for being in ministry is about following God's plan — to equip the saints for Kingdom work — and not only will it inspire you to be effective, it will also keep you going if things aren't at their best. No matter how you were called to ministry, the reality is that if you have a leadership role in reaching students with the gospel, you need to understand your purpose. Everything else springs from it.

Sometimes in order to reinforce and remember your purpose, it helps to think about when God called you into the ministry — when the Lord was speaking to you about doing something bigger — and the ways that He wanted to work through you. As you reflect on when God called you to the ministry, consider how sacred that time was between you and the Lord. You may have felt a clear, specific call, or you may have started in ministry in a more roundabout way. Whichever it was, you can probably recall how excited and scared you felt about all the Lord was doing in your life. It's these kinds of things that can give you perspective and clarity when everything in your ministry is not as smooth as you thought it would be.

It's in difficult times of struggle that we are tempted to give up and quit. It could be because someone has complained about us or someone in authority has given us a job to do that we disagree with. Sometimes we're asked to endure circumstances that are less than comfortable. If we don't reflect on the purpose of why we are in ministry and actively work to uphold our core values, it may seem like the only answer is to just do something else. I would offer this suggestion (it has worked for me, and it will work for you): Understand and work from the perspective of *why*, and you and those who help you can handle any *what* or *how*.

WHY VERSUS HOW

As pastors, we can get caught up in the "how-tos" of ministry and particulars of how a program works. We love hearing about how to grow a youth ministry and can get focused on the details of some type of step program. But is that really the starting point? I don't think so. We must develop a picture of ministry that is focused on the eternal, and as we do, we have to begin with the right perspective.

Starting with How	Starting with Why
• Focused on the calendar	• Holy Spirit led and driven
• Has a definite beginning and end	• Begins with the end/purpose in mind
• Dictated by a to-do list	• Knows where it's going but not exactly sure how God will get us there
• Man driven (about me)	• About the process or movement
• Limited by personal capabilities	• Involves everyone in the work of the ministry (about us)
• Program driven	• Starts with the leader on his or her knees in prayer
• Overly concerned with numbers rather than life-change	• Focuses on life-change — develops students instead of student ministry

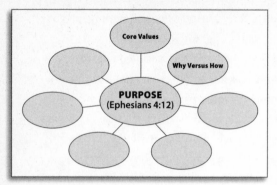

A clear purpose—and working from the right perspective—motivates and inspires not only us, but the people around us. If you want to grow a ministry, let it be defined by God-given purpose. People want to be part of something that has meaning and is going somewhere. Sure, if you throw a huge party and give away lots of things, people will show up, but will they stick around and invest themselves in God's work? Purpose allows the opportunity for students and adults to buy into the work of the ministry. That doesn't mean that throwing a big party or event is wrong, but are you going somewhere with it or are you just having an event for the sake of having an event? Take another look at the chart on page 21. Which list best describes you? If you identify more with the "how" list, are you satisfied with the constraints you've placed on your ministry by doing it all on your own or do you want to take it to another level and be involved in a movement that can only be about God? If so, then it's time to let purpose be your starting point and develop your ministry based on the "why."

CLARIFIER

Purpose is not just valuable as inspiration to keep our ministries going when it gets tough—and it will get tough—but it's also vital for a pastor in the day-to-day decisions. It offers clarity. Because purpose is tied to the philosophy of ministry, there is no way to do effective, healthy, relational ministry without understanding your purpose and keeping it foremost. Think of it this way: Purpose is the filter for every moment of the journey. When you understand how your purpose relates to everyday decisions, it gives you clarity and makes the choices easier. Whether you face meetings, staff issues, or planning programs, your purpose is not only the beginning point but also the defining force that narrows the options you have to choose from. I always liked multiple-choice

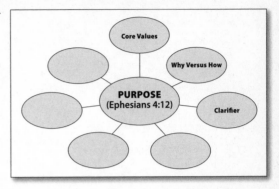

tests because usually there were a couple of answers I could discount quickly since they were so extreme. That initial elimination increased my odds of selecting the best choice from the remaining options.

Purpose can work the same way for you in ministry. When people, you included, start whining or bellyaching about something that's happening (or not happening), it's usually because they have forgotten the "why." Let's be honest; in a church full of people, not everyone will understand what you do in student ministry. In an effort to understand or help, people will propose ideas or suggestions about what kind of programs you should include or how your ministry could be more effective. Having a set purpose will answer the questions and help you evaluate the suggestions that inevitably arise. Just like answering a multiple-choice question, when you understand your purpose, you'll be able to recognize which suggestions you can immediately rule out. Of course, there will also be suggestions and ideas that do line up with the purpose and philosophy of your ministry. For those suggestions that do support the purpose and philosophy of your ministry, it's important to evaluate through prayer and wise counsel whether they are right for your ministry at this time. Remember that just because something is a good idea and matches your purpose doesn't mean it is right for your ministry at this time. We can get caught up in doing so many things that are good and yet, as Jim Collins said in *Good to Great*, "good is the enemy of great."[2] Our purpose keeps us on track and focused on choosing the more excellent way.

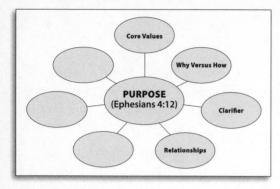

RELATIONSHIPS

Now it's time to consider the role that purpose plays on the relationships in your ministry. When you grasp the concept that youth ministry with purpose is not just about programming, but about relationships with the staff, students, workers, and parents, you will see different results. As leaders, we must be aware of the barriers that can arise and prevent us from developing strong relationships with these groups.

It's easy to put up a wall between ourselves and these groups when we get caught up in thinking that we are the pastors and therefore the only ones who know about our area of responsibility. Often we picture ourselves as the white knight riding to the rescue when something goes wrong. The problem is this mindset makes ministry all about us, building a program that revolves around and may not function without us. We begin to fall into the "how" category, and this kind of thinking makes ministry personality centered and egocentric. This is wrong and will alienate those who wish to help us fulfill God's purpose for the ministry.

I learned this lesson the hard way when I left a large church in Fort Lauderdale and went back to minister at my home church in Cleveland, Tennessee. At my first meeting with the youth workers, I spent my time telling them all I knew about ministry and "how" we were going to be doing things. As soon as I finished the meeting, a friend of mine who had been a youth worker when I was a student came to me and commented on how badly the meeting had gone. He wanted to know why I acted like I was teaching a seminar instead of being myself and warned me that if I wanted to act like an arrogant know-it-all, the ministry was going to suffer. He pointed out that

I was leading a group of people who wanted this student ministry to succeed and were willing to be on my team if I would just share the vision with them and allow them to work with me. I realized that instead of trying to show them all how much I knew, it would be much more beneficial to draw them in and work together to see what God could do through all of us.

Another barrier to developing strong relationships is that many student pastors feel constricted by those in authority over them (this could be church members or others on the staff). They tell me that they can't build an effective ministry because their plans won't be seen as acceptable to the higher-ups. That's exactly why you have to sell God's vision and purpose for your ministry to the people all around you. It's a 360-degree emphasis. When you understand your ministry philosophy and you help those around you (above and below) see what God wants to do—to grow Christ followers and Kingdom workers—then you will begin to experience buy-in from authority.

INFLUENCE

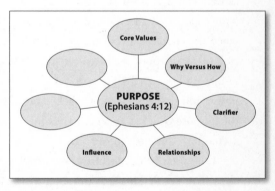

As I mentioned before, relationships in student ministry are based on four main groups of people: church staff, students, parents, and workers. Having a clearly defined purpose you believe in enables you to make it easy for these groups to catch the vision and understand what the ministry is about. This vision will cause them to be more engaged in the various aspects of all God is doing. You can't act on what you don't understand. One way we can lose influence in these groups is when we pick a program that has a beginning but an end that doesn't go anywhere. With a clearly defined purpose, the ministry is going somewhere, and it allows your people to see the goals set before them.

When a ministry is just a program or event to attend with no destination in mind, frustration creeps in to both the student pastor and the people involved in the ministry. Think of it like riding the subway all over New York City and seeing all the different stops but never having a particular place as your destination. It's pointless and frustrating (and maybe even a little dangerous). Too many youth ministers have no idea why they are doing what they are doing, and the people around them react with apathy or frustration. It is our job as leaders to embrace the purpose God has given us for ministry—equipping our students to grow in faith and help others do the same—and impart that purpose to each of the four groups.

One of the other limits to our influence and ability to sell the vision is our own lack of faith. Way too often we make ministry decisions in the dark times of life, when we are discouraged for one reason or another, and we forget to reflect on the purpose God has given us, as well as His promise to fulfill His purposes. I have seen many youth pastors who felt like God directed them in a certain way and then when the circumstances became difficult and they faced obstacles—a lack of funds, poor facilities—they lost faith and retreated from the vision. Philippians 2:13 tells us it is God who works in us, giving us the power and desire to accomplish His purposes. We must have faith in the purpose God has given us in our ministries and believe that He will accomplish that goal through us.

One time of doubt in my life occurred when I served at a large church in south Florida. Although God clearly sent me there with dreams and a vision of why I was there, the ministry was not all it should have been. I can now see that I felt intimidated, whether it was my youth or the size of the church I don't know, but this doubt in God's ability to use me in spite of the circumstances caused me to ineffectively share the vision God had given me with the pastor of the church. The result was that I became increasingly discouraged and stressed and even developed health issues. This was no one's fault but my own. Because of my fear, I failed to share the vision or dream the dream with those in authority over me. My influence as a leader was severely diminished, and the purpose God had given me was over-looked and forgotten.

It seems so simple, but in reality we can actually forget what God has said and what He has done. I never want to be guilty of that again. To make it easier to remember the Lord's promises, I have learned that if I write down these movements of God in a journal or on my computer, I will be better able to reflect and remember. These details about how the Lord moved or spoke help me when the battles of ministry come, and I'm able to find the strength to trust and con-tinue sharing the vision with those around me. We cannot be defined or limited by discouraging circumstances. By remembering God's purpose for our lives and ministries, our impact and influence will continue to grow.

RECRUITING

Notice that with the model we are using, there is no limit to where the lines of impact can occur. You will be able to see more and more areas where purpose makes a difference, like the area

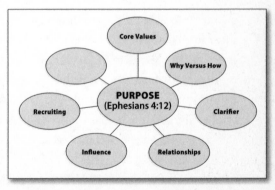

of recruiting that springs out of relationships. One of the toughest things about student ministry can be developing the leadership team and a group of consistent ministry workers.

If you feel like you need to quit or just give up, possibly you have gotten caught up in a program-centered ministry to the point that you have forgotten why you are doing ministry in the first place. That way of thinking will bleed over to the people around you, and it's probably why many youth ministers feel they are always recruiting new workers. When people understand why we do what we do, the buy-in is huge, and they'll want to take ownership in the ministry as they see where it is going. People want to be part of something that's bigger than they are. That's why when they realize there is room and a need for them within the ministry, you are no longer the only youth pastor; they become one alongside you. I always like to say, "I'm not the student pastor here, *we* are," to help remind others of their importance and reinforce the purpose of the ministry.

I remember when I first started at Long Hollow. We had about 125 students and 25 adults. I told the adults that we were going to need around 100 youth workers for the next year, because even though I had no idea who we were going to reach, students were going to come. I also told the adults that I had no idea who the additional workers would be but they did, because they knew who they wanted working alongside them. We went from approximately 25 to 85 workers that year because they went out and recruited other adults to join the team. They took ownership in the team they wanted around them. It was about more than filling slots; it was about being on a team with purpose and direction. God did a huge work through those team members, as well as in the students who took ownership in their youth group. The result was that the group of students grew from around 125 to approximately 300 that year.

As I just mentioned, the idea of recruiting and taking ownership applies not only to your adults but also to the students themselves. As we continued to see the hearts of our youth being transformed, they began bringing their lost friends to church. Their efforts eventually caused us to outgrow our space. For the past seven years we have been busing the youth off campus to a nearby high school for Sunday morning small groups. Even though we meet in the same school that many of our students attend, the groups are still growing. The students understand that God wants to work in their lives and the lives of their friends, even if that means "going to school" on a weekend. This is part of the evidence that we've effectively communicated the "why."

When students understand the purpose, they put up with inconveniences and take ownership in making Jesus famous in their communities and beyond. In fact, when I ask the question, "Who is the youth pastor at Long Hollow?" they all reply, "*We* are." This is a simple way to remind them that this ministry is about them and the purpose that God has for their lives in reaching their friends and family members with the gospel.

GROWTH

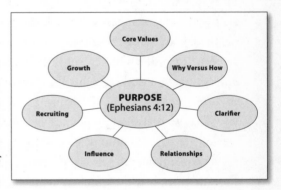

Think back to the purpose for a youth pastor and ministry that I mentioned earlier. Can you remember it? It's all about equipping the saints for the work of the ministry. Who are the saints (not the NFL team) in this case? They are the students and adults who are involved in and impacted by your ministry. It's vital that each and every group of people in your ministry feels as though they have purpose so that they take ownership in the work of the ministry. One of your main jobs as a youth pastor is to continually challenge those around you to experience the abundant life that God has for them and not to just settle for what is easy or convenient.

The greatest thing about this philosophy of ministry with purpose is that even if there is no budget, or you experience staffing issues, lack of facilities, or any other major hurdles, the ministry can still grow. I'm not just talking about growing the size of the group, although numbers are extremely important because of the lives they represent; I'm talking about spiritual growth. This spiritual growth comes about as people take ownership in the ministry and allow God to develop them as ministry leaders and transform their hearts to look continually more like Christ's.

Long Hollow has faced every major hurdle that can be faced, yet over the past seven years the student ministry has grown from approximately 150 to more than 800. We have no building. We have no room to accommodate growth in our Wednesday night program. We have no athletic facility. We bus our youth off campus just so we can all meet in the same place together. Our church attendees have an average age of about thirty-one, which means that our annual budget is significantly lower than the budgets of most churches our size. The number of youth staff we're able to employ is limited, and for many years was made up of just me and an administrative assistant. This made it even more important that the ministry not be built around me, but that the parents, youth, and workers realize they have a purpose. Even through all of these obstacles, we've still been able to witness growth in our ministry. What we don't have in physical resources we make up for in what we do have—God's purpose—and that has made all the difference.

I've mentioned the number of students our ministry has grown to, but remember, the numbers represent the lives being impacted, and that should be the purpose and focus of your ministry—to impact lives and equip the saints. For any number of reasons, the kind of numerical growth we've seen at Long Hollow may not happen everywhere, but the spiritual growth must be taking place if we want to live up to the calling God has given us to lead the next generation. Developing students and adults spiritually will reap benefits far beyond the here and now. Families today are under attack more than ever before. Think about the impact that influencing the parents in your church with the power of purpose can have on the battle for healthy families.

The Importance of Parents

Right now a few of you might be thinking about some of the "helicopter parents" you've encountered. You know, these are the parents who seem to hover over their children, worried about every step they take, possibly asking you for updates about every aspect of their kids' involvement in your ministry. This can be frustrating. But consider this: Parents can be your biggest support or your biggest obstacle. I'll admit, there have been plenty of times when I've allowed parents to become obstacles, but doesn't it make more sense to allow — even help — parents become supporters? You'll find as you do this that those helicopter parents don't feel the need to hover so much when they're involved in their children's spiritual growth.

As parents take ownership in ministry, they begin to look at their own kids in a different light. Issues that arise will take on more spiritual significance because they are no longer just parents but ministers or pastors themselves. Moms and dads will recognize ways to minister to not just their own children but also the friends of their kids. We see this happening frequently with parents who lead small groups. For one leader at our church, the students in her class continue to grow closer to her and to her daughter. As they all interact together, this parent leader has numerous opportunities to bring Jesus into conversations and influence girls with Truth. The awesome thing about this is that parents in our ministry become more intentional with not only other people's kids but with their own, so that everyday life is full of ministry moments. My own teenagers' friends have come to me for advice and encouragement because they know I care about them, and many of our parent leaders are experiencing this as well.

Not only are parents experiencing growth as they interact with students, they also are strengthened through the community that is developed when they work together. Raising teenagers is not easy, and parents need the support of one another when they encounter difficulties and raise questions. In their desire to be godly leaders and role models, parents will strive to grow in their relationships with Christ, and as they continue to grow, parents can become resources for one another, offering encouragement when needed.

When I was a youth pastor in my twenties, I know that parents of my students didn't listen to me in the same way they do now that I have three teenagers of my own. There were probably times when I came across as some young guy who thought he had the answers when in reality all I had to base my knowledge on was my own limited experience. As I am now the parent, I realize that not only do I *not* have all the answers, I have questions! This reinforces why it is so important to have parents take ownership in the ministry. They listen and talk to each other, glean from one another's experiences, and learn from those who have done it well, and even those who could have done better.

Practical Involvement

An important thing to keep in mind as you engage your team of parents and other workers is that as adults understand and feel like they have a purpose, they will want to engage in the various aspects of ministry, including leadership meetings. As you conduct leadership meetings, it is important that you not come across like you have all the answers. By keeping some answers or options open, you validate the role of your workers and engage them on even deeper levels. They will work harder to prepare lessons because the small group they lead is not yours; it's "ours." Throughout the week, they are going to stay in contact with the students in their class—text them and go to ball games or activities—because they have become the youth pastor in that class.

Two men who stand out in my mind as examples of what happens when workers live and own their purpose are Joe and Allen. They lead a small group of sixth-grade boys. You may have noticed that it can be pretty difficult to find leaders for sixth-grade boys, but Joe and Allen want to be right where they are. They both started in middle school ministry when their own children were at that stage. Their kids are long past sixth grade now, but they stay put because their purpose is to help those boys who are just entering the student ministry navigate the difficult transition from elementary to middle school.

Many sixth graders feel very uncomfortable leaving elementary school, where they were top dogs, and going to the middle school, where they are overlooked and feel like the runts of the litter. It is also a crucial year to get students plugged into the ministry. Joe and Allen are intentional about helping the young men in their small group recognize that they have a purpose and a place in ministry. They communicate that God has a plan for each person, regardless of age, and these young men come to see and believe that they have something to contribute to the Kingdom. It may be as simple as inviting some friends to church or sharing their testimonies via their social networks, but with the encouragement of Joe and Allen, these students are able to get in touch with how they can be used by God. As the boys come to understand their purpose, they leave feeling better about themselves and who they are in Christ.

Purpose leads your adults to grow personally as well as in their familial roles, and it will affect the students too. For students to take ownership in God's purpose is powerful, and the results are far reaching. They will be growing spiritually and, as they grow, they will reach their friends evangelistically, which will then make an impact in their community and beyond. When students feel like they have a purpose, they tend to be more sensitive to the call to ministry. As they begin to take ownership of God's purpose for their lives, the results are almost always growth in their faith and a deeper connection with the Holy Spirit. Often this can be seen in the way these students serve others and introduce friends to Jesus. Many may have been doing this all along and will find a renewed and refreshed energy in their service. When you effectively instill in your students the purpose of your ministry — equipping the saints — they will come to understand that as they've been participating, God has called them to continue in the ministry, either in their everyday lives or by taking on a more traditional role, possibly as a pastor, leader, or missionary.

At my first middle school camp with Long Hollow, a group of boys and I were sitting around the cabin talking about making Jesus famous at their school and beyond. They questioned whether they were too young to really do that, and I assured them that not only did I believe they were not too young but that the Bible says not to let anyone look down on us because of our age, particularly our youth (see 1 Timothy 4:12). I helped them recognize their purpose, and from that day forward they seriously owned it. They focused on their purpose and believed that they could impact others. We saw God use them to reach their campuses and their friends and to make a huge impact on our church and community.

The power of their lives was most evident when one of those very youth, Nathan, a talented athlete and musician, died suddenly. Just before his junior year of high school started, Nathan was killed in a car crash on his way to football practice. I was on vacation in upstate New York when I found out and it rocked my world. Our family was packed within a couple of hours, and we drove seventeen hours straight to reach home. Students didn't know what to do in response to the tragedy, so they began gathering at the church. Notice that they didn't gather at the school or the city park, although those were both places where Nathan was very involved. They gathered at the church, because his life was all about Jesus, and that was what felt right to them.

A few days later at his funeral, thousands of people attended the service; their lives had been touched as Nathan spent his time making Christ famous. You see, Nathan realized as a middle school student that God's purpose for him was to make Jesus famous. And he did. People across the country were impacted by Nathan, because as he went about his life, at school, at home, or even on vacation, he trusted and allowed God to use him. Because of Nathan's legacy of sharing hope with others, we honored him by inviting the people who attended his service to accept Jesus. Several were saved at the funeral that day, and I am convinced that we were able to continue to fulfill the purpose for which Nathan lived his life.

If you walk into my office, you'll see hanging on my wall the articles that were written about his life and the impact he made in his seventeen years. I often think about Nathan and remember the way he lived, because his life had purpose and he knew it. Even after his death he has reminded me of the value of purpose and why I do what I do. I hope it will encourage you as well.

These are just some examples of how living and doing ministry with purpose is vital. As you begin to apply this principle to your ministry, you will likely uncover even more reasons why it works, and then you can write the next book or just keep drawing more lines of impact on the purpose diagram. Purpose will keep you in the game and give you a reason to continue when things are tough. It will challenge others to take ownership in your ministry, and you all will experience more of what God wants to do in and through your lives.

MAKE IT LAST

Use the transformation questions to move the principle of purpose from the pages of this book to your daily life and ministry.

1. Reflect on the time when God led you into the ministry. How would you describe what you thought and felt at that time?

2. Take an index card, and on one side list five feelings you had when you were first called to or started in ministry. On the back, list five feelings you are experiencing today. Consider the reasons these two lists might be similar or different and write a brief explanation here.

3. Identify your purpose as a pastor.

4. Would you say that purpose is foundational to your ministry at this point in time? Why or why not?

5. Using a scale of 1 to 5 (5 being "They take ownership," and 1 being "It's all on me"), rate the following groups of people:

_____ Students
_____ Workers
_____ Parents

Understand that if you answered "yes" to question 4, yet your groups in question 5 rated low, it's possible your ministry doesn't have as much purpose as you think; it might be built around you.

6. What one thing will you start doing immediately to strengthen the purpose of your ministry?

CHAPTER 2

DEVELOP A WINNING GAME PLAN

Winning teams don't just know that their purpose is to win, they have a well-developed game plan designed to achieve victory. Every great leader and organization does the same. If you are really interested in developing a student ministry that is healthy, growing, and effective, the next step after understanding your purpose is to focus on your plan. As you begin, the right question to ask is "How will I go about the daily business of student ministry so that the purpose is accomplished?" In this chapter I will share with you some specifics I've learned along the way that make the concept of "working a plan" simple to put into place in your ministry today.

The reality is that you must have a plan of action for how you will lead the ministry God has given you or it will be in trouble. Without a well-thought-out and prayed-over plan, your student ministry could easily become a time for video-game competitions, and your ability to build relationships with students and adults could be limited to the interactions that take place across various social networks. While these things may have a place, if you want to have an effective student ministry, it will involve developing a plan that encompasses much more than Facebook and video games.

DEVELOPING AND COMMUNICATING THE PLAN

So where does a plan come from? Unfortunately, I can't give you the magic outline. Your ministry plan will be unique to you, your style, and the dreams and passion that God has laid on your heart. As you develop your plan, it is vital that you start with what you discover from the Lord about His plans for you and build off your purpose and core values. Once you understand what your personal philosophy of student ministry is, you will begin to see the necessary steps for making that ministry happen. If your philosophy is a small group–driven ministry, then you will most likely start by recruiting and training a group of leaders for those small groups. If your philosophy is an event-driven ministry, then you will study the calendar for key times in the year to hold events that can impact both students and the community. Your focus will be on what types of events to hold and finding key speakers and bands to fulfill your purpose. Remember to seek wise counsel from key students and adults in your ministry as you develop your plan so that it will take into account the climate and culture in which you serve.

As you're developing your ministry plan, keep in mind that a plan must be easy to communicate. Ease of communication is not only so that you can explain it but so others can explain it for you. Many student pastors may be tempted to make a complicated, involved plan of how to do ministry and achieve goals with the mistaken belief that it will make them look smarter or more in control. Often the exact opposite happens, so the best plans are simple and easy to understand as well as communicate.

Once you have a simple, easy-to-communicate plan, you must learn to sell the plan. As a student pastor you need to think about how you will market the plan and then (to borrow a concept from sales) how you will close the plan. It is important that you finish with this "closing the plan" step since this is where you will ask the other person to make a commitment to the ministry and they will agree to become involved in whatever you're asking them to do. Why does this matter?

It goes back to the purpose of equipping the saints to do the work of the ministry. This can only happen when you understand that the people involved have to buy into the plan in order for you to multiply your ministry. Many youth pastors work hard at selling the plan but stop short of asking for the commitments necessary to reflect their buy-in of the plan.

This buy-in starts with the senior pastor and the way you market the plan to those on staff who have authority over you. When you think about your plan, think: clear, concise, and focused. You want the senior pastor (and anyone else) to be able to articulate the plan back to you. I remember a time early in my ministry when I didn't really understand this concept. Although I knew the easy things I could do to make ministry happen, most of those were based on my skills and not necessarily a well-thought-out and effective plan. This didn't necessarily hurt me or my ministry there, but it caused me some serious issues at the next church where I served. Since I hadn't learned to develop and sell my ministry plan, I was unable to get the pastor to understand my vision of ministry. When you learn to develop and communicate your ministry plan, it will help you to understand and believe in your purpose, your plan, and yourself better. Your ministry will be more productive and have a lasting effect, and you will save yourself some serious heartache along the way. These same principles are true of each person you sell your plan to. You want them to own, understand, and be able to articulate the plan. Why? Because when they do, you'll know you have their buy-in, and that's what the plan needs.

Selling your plan to the authority on staff is vital, but it is just the beginning. You also need to communicate the plan to the other groups of people involved — students, workers, and parents. No group should be overlooked. Selling your plan to the students is the part of this chapter that some of you are already doing. Many student pastors mistakenly think that as long as the students are on the same page, that's all there is to worry about. In reality, the other three groups mentioned are just as important, if not more, because when the adults around you understand the *why* and they understand your plan, they enable you to do the work of the ministry more effectively.

Over the years I've learned to sell my plan to my pastor as well as others, but each student pastor must develop their own style of communicating the plan. The way the plan is developed may differ but some elements will be the same in an effective, enduring plan.

WORKING THE PLAN

First, the plan must be talked about all the time. All the time. This means that you are moving the people from the *why* to the *how*. They have understood the purpose of what you are building and now they need to grasp how it's going to be accomplished. When we had the challenge of moving the students at Long Hollow off campus in order to create more space for groups, I first had to sell the idea to the pastor. I then took him with me to meet with the workers in order to sell the plan to them. By the time that meeting was over, the workers were completely on board and ready to go for it. We did the same thing when meeting with the parents about the concept, and the results were the same. From that point on I had all those other adults—parents, workers, and the pastor—helping to sell the plan. This eased my burden and made the transition much smoother.

When a plan has been communicated and sold to the people around you, it will be talked about. I like to say, "Talk about it early and often." You have to continually keep the plan in the front of people's minds. Anytime something happens that lines up with your purpose and plan, make a big deal about it. This could mean anything from announcing what took place from the pulpit, making it known at Wednesday night services, or taking someone to coffee to celebrate life-change. This isn't about bringing glory or accolades to you; it's about reinforcing and legitimizing your God-given plan of ministry.

If you neglect to talk about it when something great happens and you don't make a big deal about it, no one has any idea that your ministry plan is working. If those around you fail to see an effective plan and haven't built any trust in it, it's more likely that you will take the blame when something goes wrong. When you learn to make a big deal about the positive things happening in your ministry, people will begin to trust you and your plan.

I can guarantee that things will not always go perfectly, so it matters that you have built trust through your plan. This truth applies to both little and big accomplishments. If someone gets saved at your Wednesday night service because one student brought a friend, then let people know and invite them to rejoice with you. Consequently, when the buses are late or the crowd is down, if everyone is engaged in the plan and the process, they will shoulder the burden alongside you. You will have others to help discern what needs to change and improve. As you continue to talk about and implement the plan, those involved will take on a "we" mentality, meaning each person becomes the student pastor; it won't all revolve around you. This is exactly what our plan should be helping us accomplish. When there's a "we" mentality in our ministry, everyone can celebrate the good things as well as shoulder the burdens.

The next thing to consider while working the plan is that it must be intentional. It can't focus only on outreach or become solely incarnational; it must flow inside out *and* outside in. Although it's easy to get caught up in which style is better, both are necessary for an effective, intentional plan. If you are wondering why, then think about this: A plan that is just about outreach or events focuses on gathering people and moving toward life-change. The temptation with this is that the individual may be overlooked within the group. An incarnational ministry can best be described as taking ministry from the inside out and focusing on inner transformation to become "like Christ." The temptation with this style is that people become self-focused and overlook those who need to be reached. There is no need for competition between the different styles, and each person can and should play a part in the larger plan.

As student pastors, we must be intentional about bringing people to Christ. Remember that it can't just be about us as individuals, because Jesus came to seek and save those who are lost. His plan was about reaching those who didn't know Him, and our plan must do the same. It takes focus and intentionality to lead this kind of ministry. There have been times in my ministry when I wasn't intentional about what we were doing, and I just did something because it was on the calendar. This happened early on when I was the new student pastor and had been handed a calendar of events for the coming year. It was clear that I was expected to carry on with the events, and I didn't always evaluate them. I should have considered each event through the grid of my plan. Had I done that, I could have prayerfully determined whether an event would reinforce and move the plan forward as part of my ministry purpose or if it was just something to do.

Although I had been intentional and purposeful about ministry before, I didn't have a specific grid that I could use for evaluation of ministry until I came to Long Hollow in 2002. My friend and executive pastor—who had been the student pastor before me—Lance Taylor challenged me to be more intentional about evaluation. He gave me a grid to filter everything through, and I added this evaluation aspect to my plan. By pairing a plan that was easy to market, easy to sell, intentional, and easy to communicate, the process of evaluation became greatly simplified. The grid on page 43 is what Lance introduced me to that changed my ministry, and I'm convinced it will help your ministry become even more effective.

The filter that was designed to be the strategy and purpose grid for our student ministry at Long Hollow soon became the overall strategy of Long Hollow as a church. With some tweaking along the way, this filter has served us well in our student ministry because it challenges us to evaluate the way we do staffing, budgeting, and all other aspects of ministry. When we study the grid, we see where we are out of balance and what we need to work on. You can see the different parts listed on the next page to better understand what I am talking about.

EVENTS

	Idea 1	Idea 2	Idea 3	Idea 4	Idea 5	Idea 6
Come to Worship						
Connect in Fellowship						
Grow in Discipleship						
Serve Others in Ministry						
Go Reach the World						

FILTERS

As you read the grid, you might notice that the filters cover different purposes as outlined in Scripture and written about in various books over the years. We've just developed our own terminology. As we walk through each aspect of the filter, you will see not only how and why it should be part of your ministry but also where it is found in Scripture. The order of the list is not accidental. There is a funnel type of approach in dealing with things in this order. It moves from the masses or large groups of people to the individual. Let's break down each category to give you an idea of what it involves.

COME TO WORSHIP

The entry point of "Come to Worship" involves what is typically a person's introduction to our student ministry or church. In Hebrews 10:25, we find the challenge to not forsake meeting together, and that's the premise behind these "Come" events. An effective student ministry will make worship and gathering together a big deal because these are some of the easiest times for people to be introduced to your ministry. These events are also a great time of growth and encouragement for group members.

These larger worship events are usually services that channel the masses (or at least a lot of people) toward the Savior. Our Wednesday night worship service for middle school students is called The Current. Our high school worship service is River's Edge. These are the weekly "Come" opportunities, but we also include several other "Come" opportunities throughout the year, such as:

- A student crusade in the fall, which is a four-day worship/evangelistic event that reaches all ages of youth in large numbers.
- Quest, which is similar to a Disciple Now weekend experience, in which students stay in church homes with college leaders.

- Youth camp, an intense week in the summer that covers
  multiple purposes. This event allows us to reach a ton of lost
  students who come to camp with their friends. Students get
  to spend some incredible time in fellowship as they grow in
  their understanding of the Word of God and in their
  relationships with Christ. Camp can also be considered
  missions since our students introduce their friends to Christ
  while they are experiencing camp together.

While these are some of the staple "Come" opportunities our student ministry hosts each year, we are always open to fun, fresh, creative ideas that will bring students together. In coming together we
can build relationships with them, and through those relationships we
are able to share Christ with them. Our goal is for students to get to
know us and see who we are as a ministry. We want the unchurched to
realize that "church" is not about the building but about the people
who do life together. Whether we hold our events at the church building, at a local school, or in neighborhoods, we are always looking for
entry points to reach people.

One example of a fun way to reach people that we have had huge
success with is a dodgeball tournament. We challenge our students to
build dodgeball teams using four or five church friends and four or five
lost friends. They then enter their team in a tournament and make team
names and creative uniforms for themselves. The first year we hosted
this outreach, it drew in about two thousand students from all ages and
schools in our area. (In case you're wondering how we host that many
people, we use the local football field and divide it into dodgeball
courts.) Big cash prizes were given to the winning teams. Our first-place
prize was $500, and $250 was given to the second-place team. Don't
freak out over the prize money. Early in my ministry I would have
spent more money than that on a pizza party. We've noticed that by
offering cash prizes, more students were interested in participating.

When students arrived at the tournament, we recorded each

person's contact information as part of registration. We didn't ask for any money from the students, and our investment was minimal. Because we involved our adult workers from the beginning stages and were able to effectively convey how this event helped fulfill the purpose of our ministry, we had more volunteers than we could put to work. Remember, the more adults and students you involve in organizing your "Come" opportunities, the more people you will reach.

We began the event with a large group assembly in the gym of the school to give instructions *and* a clear presentation of the gospel. Many students prayed to receive Christ that night. Even though they came to play dodgeball, they heard the truth about Jesus and their need for Him. This was the most important part, as well as the success, of the event. It wasn't about the thousands of students who participated in the games of dodgeball; it was the fact that many people — students and adult volunteers — were introduced to Jesus, and He touched hearts and drew them to Himself. This outcome is the type of thing that should be celebrated as part of your ministry plan and remembered as you evaluate future events with the help of the grid.

Understand that some of the events I am describing will actually fall into more than one category of the grid. For instance, Quest is an event that falls under "Come," "Grow," "Connect," and even "Go" because of the service projects that occur. Think about this: Whenever an event can wear multiple tags from the grid, it is even more intentional in the ministry plan. But the key to using the grid is that if a prospective event does not fit into any of the grid categories, it does not make the cut and we don't invest time or resources.

The key to turning your special events into multiple grid categories is to be more intentional in the planning and promotional stages. Something like youth camp, typically a "Connect" and "Grow" event, can be turned into a "Come" event, which means that the lost and unchurched are big participants.

It may help for you to see what we do in our ministry to make camp very intentional. If you plan a similar event, I'd encourage you and your leadership team to:

- Develop an overall theme and direction of what you want to see accomplished at camp.
- Set goals for the number of students you want to involve. Be sure that the goal is large enough to challenge everyone to be involved (it's the mentality of "It can only happen if we *all* do our part"). The goal must also be attainable. It's important to find the balance between stretching yourselves and being realistic.
- Challenge each student to bring five friends to camp (this can help you estimate a possible goal for the total number of student attendees).
- Contact sports teams and encourage them to bring their whole team.
- Plan for the number of adults needed according to the student goal. (We keep a 1:6 adult to student ratio so that the time remains relational.)
- Involve everyone (students, adults, workers, parents, staff, and even the pastor) in recruiting and inviting students to come to camp.
- Raise scholarship money from the church so that youth who can't afford the week are able to come. This makes it possible for those who cannot volunteer their time to be involved in the good things God does at camp.
- Ask those at home to wear prayer bracelets and lift up a specific person at camp all week (praying for students, leaders, volunteers, and speakers).

Over the past nine years, our church as a whole has embraced this concept and philosophy of camp to the point that our first goal was to have 150 students attend, and nine years later the goal is around

1,400. That's a lot of life-change. The church staff has bought into this completely, and the senior pastor comes to camp and teaches our morning Bible study.

A great way to keep everyone (students, staff, and other adults) involved in the excitement of what God is doing in your ministry is to have a Camp Celebration Service back home after camp is over. The service is a time to show video from camp, share testimonies from students and adults, and baptize those students and adults who gave their lives to Christ at camp. One year we baptized 181 people and at the end of the service, we offered an invitation to those present who wanted to give their hearts to Christ; many came forward to do so that night.

We've heard testimonies from many who've attended these events. One student who gave his life to Christ at camp brought someone else with him the next year who then accepted Jesus. Later, those two talked to a guy who worked with them. He came to the Camp Celebration Service and decided to follow Jesus. It happens all the time, and just as I mentioned earlier, we celebrate every decision for Christ!

These are just a couple examples, and not an exhaustive list, of different outreach events you might consider. It has been exciting to see how God has used "Come" events like these to reach scores of students and their families and the community at large.

CONNECT IN FELLOWSHIP

The second purpose listed on the grid is "Connect in Fellowship." Fellowship is all about relationships, both with the Lord and with others. It's about living in a unified body of people who have a common interest: becoming Christlike and serving in the Kingdom. Acts 2:42 tells us that believers of the early church devoted themselves to fellowship. Just as they were committed to fellowship, we, too, must take it seriously.

"Connect" is all about ways we fellowship and do life together in student ministry. Our strategy is not about compartmentalizing the different aspects of life. When an adult comes to me and shares how she observed some of the teenagers from our ministry at a local store going out of their way to assist a lady they didn't know with her packages because the basket on her motorized chair was too small, I realize that some students are understanding this concept. Another example of teens who are "getting it" would be the comments I hear from coaches and teachers in the local public schools telling me about how students involved in our ministry behave at school. I heard about one young man who got up from his seat in class to walk across the room and help a fellow student pick up the things from her dropped backpack while everyone else just snickered and laughed. We want this kind of selflessness to be the norm for all our students.

Too many students, and adults, have one way they live at church and a different set of standards for work or school. This is not consistent with the way that believers are called to live, and it's not effective as a witness. As you consider how your ministry plan will help students connect in fellowship, think about how you can help them take a holistic approach to their lives. Talk about the flow of life or doing life together, always keeping in mind the purpose of building relationships along the way. Doing life together means supporting and encouraging one another while holding each other accountable. When we train and lead our students and adults to live out their faith in the things they are doing as part of everyday life at school, work, home, or with friends, we are developing an effective ministry. This leads to deeper relationships with one another and a better sense of belonging. The world is watching believers to see if their lives reflect what they say they believe. Authenticity is attractive, and when other people see the life-change Jesus is causing in you and in your students, they will want what you have; it's a chain reaction.

Often in the church world, we miss out on connecting in

fellowship because we aren't intentional about it. We don't even talk about it much. We have the "build it and they will come" mentality. That is not the way Jesus lived. He made disciples as He went about His life and took the time to develop relationships, investing time and prayer in those around Him. Just as Jesus made disciples, we are told to make disciples as we go, but we cannot forget that the relationships we form with those around us must be purposeful. That is our focus of fellowship and doing life together.

GROW IN DISCIPLESHIP

Most churches have a goal of making disciples. Scripture commands us all to go and make disciples (see Matthew 28:19). Once we understand that, the question becomes "How do we make disciples?" Just as people learn differently, disciples are also made in vastly different ways. Discipleship is more than Bible study. That doesn't take away or minimize the need for studying the Bible, because that's a valuable discipline for spiritual growth, but discipleship is also about putting students into various situations that provide multiple environments and opportunities for them to grow in their personal relationship with Christ. Whether it's a small group where they learn together and experience accountability or a mission trip where they have opportunities to apply God's Word, get their hands dirty as they serve others, and stretch their boundaries, the goal is to help them allow the Holy Spirit to work in their lives.

My desire is for students to learn to grow and disciple themselves by the work of the Holy Spirit so that they can truly own their faith. People who disciple themselves have learned how to grow in their faith without being dependent on someone else. These students are the ones who go off to college and even though they don't have parents waking them up for an early-morning Bible study or their student pastor encouraging them to participate, they stay strong in their faith because they have owned it. Not learning to push and disciple themselves is one of the main reasons students leave the faith when they are no longer involved with student ministry. If we continually place students in circumstances that allow them to develop their relationship with the Holy Spirit, their faith becomes dependent on the Holy Spirit instead of other people.

Challenging our students to own their faith doesn't deny the importance of other people—mentors, teachers, and leaders. If you truly want to see students own their faith in your student ministry, then who you place in leadership roles around the students is crucial to helping them grow. Cultivate leaders who ask the right questions, model a biblical worldview, and teach your students to really think, not just repeat facts. The right leaders will help students learn to trust and rely on the Spirit for all aspects of life.

Another common misconception about how to help students own their faith is that they should be cocooned within the church environment, associating only with like-minded people and other believers. The truth is, most people learn best from reflecting on experiences and mistakes they have made. That's not to say that we would want to encourage students to sin, but we in the church have sometimes robbed them of the opportunity to really examine themselves—their convictions and faith—by refusing to raise the bar spiritually. Students cannot test themselves if we continually spoon feed and belittle them, undermining their confidence in the Holy Spirit's ability to help them stand up under temptation and minister to people in their lives.

SERVE OTHERS IN MINISTRY

"Serve" is the next layer of the purpose grid. It is fairly self explanatory. Serving is all about doing something for others or helping meet someone else's needs. This generation of students has a strong desire to serve and feel useful. They want to see the before and after of ministry, and they take seriously Jesus' command to love our neighbors as we love ourselves (see Matthew 22:39). At Long Hollow we try to offer numerous opportunities for students to serve—helping in the preschool, loading luggage for trips, setting up before services, or participating in organized community-service days. There are as many ways to serve as there are personalities of students.

One of our favorite yearly "Serve" opportunities happens at a major "Come" event. Many churches across the country do weekend events called Disciple Now (D-Now). No matter the name, it's a weekend, in-home retreat where small groups of students stay at homes with leaders, then meet together at the church for large-group worship times. For years I worked hard to come up with creative things for students to do on Saturday afternoon. We did video scavenger hunts, athletic competitions, and anything else we thought would entertain them. When we began using Saturday afternoon for service projects, we saw a huge increase in the students' interest level. Instead of the afternoon being just a random part of the whole weekend, it became a drawing point and one of their favorite aspects of the D-Now weekend.

As we develop a vision for our ministry plan, many times we are very creative in planning our worship or "Come" events, but we sometimes overlook the need to be creative in our "Serve" opportunities. Service is a key way to draw in students and enable them to own the ministry as well as their faith. You can involve students in other creative "Serve" opportunities by asking them to volunteer at church-wide events. This became clear to me when I served at First Baptist Church of Fort Lauderdale and saw scores of young people serving food to the homeless on the streets of downtown during the Feast of Plenty. On one day around Thanksgiving, our church fed more than five thousand meals to the homeless. The students were a key part. They started the night before, helping set up tables on the blocked-off road, and then served meals, escorted homeless people to their tables, talked with the people, and shared the gospel. I was in my mid-twenties when I experienced that and recognized the need to create and find opportunities for students to serve regularly. That event also reinforced the reality that student ministry is not just about the leader but about the students becoming the ministers too.

There is no limit to what students can do to serve others in ministry. If you need creative ideas, ask them. Check with your church members to see where some needs are, and then match small groups of students with those needs. Our students wash cars for single moms at an event held just for them, rake leaves and do yard work for senior adults, watch kids for single moms or dads, paint rooms at ministry houses, and collect diapers for the crisis pregnancy center. Never underestimate the potential of your students to serve and impact others.

GO REACH THE WORLD

"Go Reach the World" encompasses missions from the inside out. Think of it as going from the neighborhood to the nations as described in Acts 1:8. Our goal is for students to think in terms of reaching their neighbors, their ball teams, their clubs, their bands, their schools, and anyone else God brings across their paths. If we are intentional about leading our students to be mission-minded, then we will increasingly see more life-change, because it is students who reach students most effectively. Recognize that students are living life together, and as they do that, their lost or unchurched peers will be influenced. Students are sometimes more open to hearing certain things from another student who has gone through similar circumstances than from an adult they feel can't relate. I see this so clearly when I invite uninvolved students to an event and they don't show much interest in ever attending. It's a different story when I send one of our involved students to invite them to the same event. They are more willing to commit to something that their peers are doing because I'm the adult who is *supposed* to invite them and their friend is *choosing* to put his reputation on the line for whatever it is they'll be attending together. One thing I have noticed, and believe you will see as well, is that once students get a taste of missions and being used by God, they won't be satisfied with less.

Why and How to Reach the Schools

Reaching the schools in our area is a huge focus of our student ministry. At my first church in Louisiana, getting into the schools to build relationships was fairly easy. That was probably in part due to the atmosphere in the South and the culture as a whole. I've found that other places are not always as welcoming when it comes to developing relationships between the church and the schools in the area. It's not always easy, but it is worth it. In starting a school ministry it's vital that you begin with the administration and work your way down to the students. The administration can open doors for you, and they can shut doors. It was easy to build this type of relationship in Louisiana because the school administrators wanted and needed help. Those in our ministry earned their trust. We were able to be chaplains to teams, take watermelon to football practice, and so on.

When I moved to south Florida, things were very different. The public schools weren't nearly as welcoming, and we had to challenge our students to take ownership of reaching their friends in the schools. I remember going to a school and talking with the principal to receive permission for us to visit with the students and talk to them during lunch. He refused and said, "We don't do that kind of thing around here." As I was leaving, I noticed that the school was in a campaign to raise money for their weight room. I consulted with some business-men and the students at that school. By working together we raised some money to go toward the school's campaign. When I was able to present the principal of the school with a check to support the project, he began to look at me as a person who was on his team and not an outsider coming in with all the answers. It opened the door for us to build necessary relationships.

Once I understood the importance of building relationships with administrators in schools and challenging our students and workers to do the same, the opportunities to "Go" in our community enlarged. Having learned that lesson in Florida, in my current ministry I don't like to think of "Go" as separated out into different parts of the community. It's much more effective to view "Go Reach the World" through the lens of how we go about our daily lives and do life together.

When I came to Long Hollow, our student ministry was already feeding meals to the local high school football team before their games. I went to the principal to talk about how we could become more involved and supportive of the school. He wasn't sure what I was talking about, so I asked when they were having their next teacher gathering. He responded that their next faculty in-service day was the following week. I asked if we could prepare and serve a nice dinner for his staff and teachers for free. Of course he said yes, and I didn't ask for anything in return. My goal was not to talk to the group or anything but just to support and encourage the school. After that dinner, I asked the principal if we could feed some of the other teams, and he agreed. We expanded our school ministry into other schools nearby, and now we have four local high schools that we are involved with through feeding teams and have built trust with the schools, principals, and faculty. You are probably wondering where the money for things like that comes from. It's simple; parents and adults in the community see school outreach as a "Go" opportunity and they contribute in whatever ways they can. We've found that when God has directed us to serve our communities as part of our ministry plan, He always blesses our efforts.

Our ministry also has ongoing relationships with several middle schools, and we currently allow the county to use our church facility to do their county-wide teacher in-service days. They do their own training, but we serve as hosts. We also allow the high schools to use our facility to hold their graduation ceremonies. You may question how you could possibly do that in your community. It takes time to build trust and relationships. Look for ways to minister to and serve the schools. We never view the schools as adversaries but as partners with us. As they educate the students, we try to minister to and serve them because they're on our team. When you aren't welcomed by the school the first time you go there, look for strategic ways to serve them and earn their trust. Pick up trash, paint the bathrooms, feed a ball team, make over the teachers' lounge, stay after ball games and clean up the stadium. Don't preach at them. Whether you serve at the local schools or the local ballparks, let them see your love by your service.

From Neighborhoods to the Nations

Our "Go" opportunities are designed by age and stage. Everyone does community missions. As the trips expand out from the church, different groups are the focus for filling the trip teams. Regional trips are for middle school students, national trips are geared toward high schoolers, and international trips are for older high school and college students.

While planning your missions, it's important to develop partnerships. As the leaders, we must be intentional about finding those partnerships. Partners can range from local churches in need of help to regional or international organizations you have researched and respect. In our ministry, we go and do missions in different areas according to what the people of those areas share about the needs there. In some places, our students may hold Vacation Bible Clubs or block parties. Our students have walked through neighborhoods praying for the residents and cleaned up prospective church buildings. We have been involved with hosting and leading wilderness camps for underprivileged children, giving them the chance to sleep in tents and enjoy a typical outdoor camping experience. The possibilities are endless, and those we've partnered with guide us in the planning of these trips. We depend on and trust them. Why? Because they are the people who are there day in and day out. Too many churches tell a community, "We are coming to help you, and this is what we are going to do." We could inform a local church plant that we will be coming in and holding block parties to help spread the word about their ministries, but they may know that those types of things have not been well received in their area for some reason. Allowing the residents of the area to tell us what is needed is much more effective.

As you consider the plan and filter of Come, Connect, Grow, Serve, and Go, hopefully you've found it to be simple and effective just as I do. Using a filter or grid will enable you to do what I talked about early in this chapter: work the God-given plan at the place you have been called. It might look a little different for you, and many events and activities will fit within more than one aspect of the grid—but remember that's good, because overlap only strengthens the plan.

It's vital that when you have a God-given purpose, you don't settle for an ordinary plan but always work through a God-sized plan. We don't want to be in a church where we can explain away everything that happens; we want to be part of a ministry that can only be explained with the knowledge that "God did it." God alone deserves the credit, so only God should receive the credit.

MAKE IT LAST

Use the transformation questions in this section to evaluate how your ministry's plan will support your purpose.

1. What is your plan for ministry? How do you go about the daily business of student ministry so that the purpose is accomplished?

2. Who have you communicated the plan to? Are there other groups of people you might still need to communicate the plan to? List them here and write a brief description of how you plan to approach each group.

3. Is your plan easy for you and others to communicate? If not, how will you change it?

4. Of the five purposes on the grid, which is a strength in your ministry? Which is a weakness? Come up with three ideas of how your ministry can improve in its area of weakness.

CHAPTER 3

PAINT THE PICTURE

It's been said that a picture is worth a thousand words. Too often in ministry we overlook this concept and spend a lot of time talking, talking, talking. Although communication is certainly important, and as we discussed in chapter 2 it definitely involves talking, images are also important. The concept of this enduring principle is that as part of communicating your ministry's purpose and plan, you have to learn to *paint a picture* for your people.

Images can be powerful motivators. When we hear people talking, our minds create images that correlate with what we are hearing. Your job as the student pastor is to communicate in such a way that your hearers paint a picture that matches the picture you have of your plan.

Jesus offers us wonderful examples of this principle. He spent time telling stories, motivating people, and inspiring them to move, react, or respond. Jesus was the master storyteller, and He painted pictures for people through stories that always had a higher purpose.

PAINTING PICTURES THROUGH STORIES

One aspect of Jesus' storytelling that works for us as well is that He often used stories to help people see what could and should be. Whether He spoke to groups or individuals, the stories Jesus used were effective in helping others see their lives differently. They were able to paint a picture from Jesus' words that gave them a goal and an image to move toward.

In ministry leadership, we must learn to paint a picture for our people of what effective ministry or, in essence, the plan looks like. You may know and be able to see the picture, but they don't have access to your mind. Don't be the leader who thinks as long as you see the goal, everyone else can just follow your instructions. That kind of thinking leads to the opposite of everyone buying into and becoming part of the ministry. Our goal is to follow the example of Christ. Jesus didn't hold the plan inside of Him. He knew His audience and shared stories and parables with them in such a way that they could relate and respond to His leadership. They saw the picture.

This principle was missing early in my ministry. Even if I had a purpose and a plan to some degree, I sometimes failed to paint the picture to the pastor and staff. By not painting the picture for them, I limited the amount of ownership they could take in the vision and kept it from being a shared vision. Sometimes we, as leaders, become possessive of our vision, and we want to own it. That's what I did until I realized that God's plan is much bigger than me. Since we are each part of the body of Christ, the vision must be shared.

As you paint the picture of your ministry plan for those around you, they will begin to see the vision for themselves, from their own perspectives. Their perceptions of that picture can then enhance your own view of it. This is much like the body of Christ. Each person has a role to play, and each will see the picture through their own lens.

I was able to see how powerful this concept is once when I was chaplain at the University of Tennessee. It was the year after they had won a national championship in football, and I was speaking to the leaders of the team. I challenged the returning players to paint a picture for the new players on the team of what it looks like to win a national championship, including what it takes to achieve that goal. The returning players held the key to sharing the vision with the newer players, and the same is true in ministry. Each year the dynamics are different on a team and in a ministry. Therefore, the responsibility falls on the shoulders of those of us who are more experienced in the process to paint the picture of what the journey will look like for those who are just coming alongside us or joining the team. It is a unifying and team-strengthening exercise.

VISION MEETINGS

Another aspect of painting the picture for people is to engage in meetings to develop the vision. It's important to have set times with the people around you in order to talk about the development of the picture you have been sharing. You can also allow time for others to share any pictures they hold inside themselves. These need to be intentional moments when you ask those around you to clarify and share how they see different things happening or evolving in your ministry.

I once heard that knowledge is reflected in the answers you give and wisdom in the questions you ask. When we learn to ask good questions about the vision and goal of our ministry, we will gain much wisdom and clarity for the everyday issues. It will affect not only us as we lead but those who are involved in our ministry.

Recently, our church was hit with some very hard and sad news about some of the orphans we sponsor and had built an orphan village for in Haiti. Our pastor was preparing to shoot an informational video to send out online as a call to prayer for the people. One of the executive staff asked me what I thought the pastor should say, and my response was this question: "What do you see happening as a result of this video?" In other words, I encouraged him to paint a picture of what he wanted to accomplish, and then we could work backward to develop the video in order to make the picture a reality. Helping people see vision and learn to articulate it needs to be an intentional part of your leadership style.

The following are a few questions you can ask during vision meetings:

- How do you see that aspect of ministry working out?
- What would you say is the goal of
  _____?
- In one sentence, what do you want to accomplish through
  _____?
- What, if anything, would you do differently to see this picture come to fruition?

Asking these questions can change your life and ministry. The people around you will be more engaged, and your ministry will be stronger. As a young pastor in ministry, I was gung ho and going, going, going. I wasn't intentional about sharing the vision or plan, and I didn't paint the picture so that others could be involved. During that time I missed the concept of asking questions and expanding the picture as I worked hard and did it all myself. Now that I've learned to paint the picture and involve others in the work of the ministry, God is showing me greater things He can do in and through the ministry.

DIFFERENT STROKES

Everyone is not the same kind of learner. Some people can perfectly picture things they hear described, others can't. If I call a play in football, such as a sweep to the wide side of the field, some can see that instantly, while others may need to have it drawn out on a board, while still others, like my wife, are trying to figure out what a sweep is and how you can tell which side of the field is wide. In order to effectively paint the picture for your people, sometimes it's necessary to *actually paint the picture.*

"Painting the picture" can be done by using a concept called story-boarding. You can do this by combining the spoken words with a projector and screen to display the concept to the audience. Today's technology has no limits; you can get very creative in the ways you paint the picture and share the vision. If you understand the basics of storyboarding, you can use them in many different technological ways. In storyboarding, you give images to the variety of things that need to happen at an event in order to achieve the final results you desire.

Pretend you are planning an event. What needs to happen at the event? What is the end goal? You create a board that will take you from where you are now to the final goal or vision of what you desire to see happening. You can also work backward to achieve the desired result. This involves deciding what the end goal looks like and then creating the different pictures or slides that will help you achieve that goal. Here is an example of how you might storyboard the dodgeball event I described in chapter 2.

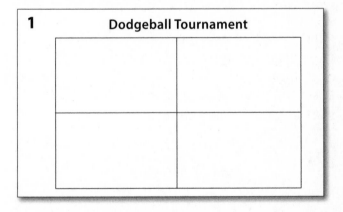

Here you can see that Frame 1 shows the location of the dodgeball tournament. By dividing the field into four parts, you can show and explain that there will be at least four courts for simultaneous games. Remember, your pictures do not have be an exact representation of what will take place. They just need to convey the overall idea.

The picture of Frame 2 shows not only that you will need volunteers, but why. The line of people approaching the table represents those who will be registering for the event. It's up to the leader to explain to the ministry team where they will find the volunteers and how to explain the purpose of the tournament to them.

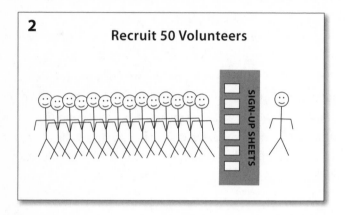

Frame 3 represents getting the word out about the event. You can explain to your team how you'll advertise for the event (flyers, e-mails, posters, word of mouth). The heading can be as specific or generic as you'd like. This particular heading specifies the number of students you'd like to sign up for the tournament.

The last frame in this storyboard depicts the ultimate purpose of the event: presenting the gospel to the participants and volunteers.

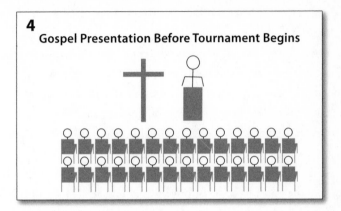

As you begin creating the storyboard, consider starting with your goal and developing the other pictures after. Whether you begin with the idea of the starting point or work backward beginning with the ultimate goal, remember that this will be a brief representation of what you are planning. Your pictures can be as in-depth or basic as you'd like but will only represent the major steps of the process, since later you'll be explaining each step to your team and can go into more detail then.

START EARLY

No matter what route you take to paint the picture, whether it's by telling stories or using images as in storyboarding, the end goal is the same. You want people to see the plan as a picture in their mind and heart. They will then take ownership of the plan and will become more passionate about it. Once this happens, they will be able to minster alongside you in their passion. Your first few months at a church are so vital because it's during this time that you start to dream the plan with the people around you by painting a picture of what it looks like. This involves them in the ministry and allows them to help you see how the plan might work best in that particular culture and climate.

If you have ever been like me and missed out on this principle, you will recognize that without painting the picture, your ministry will be limited. I have seen this evidenced in my early ministry. When I overlooked the concept of painting the picture, I fell into the trap of making ministry all about me. I went out and did ministry all on my own since I was the only one who could see the picture. People would even say things like "Look how good Jeff is at ministry" or "He is doing such a great job." These comments felt good at the time, but that mentality led to a very limited ministry.

In all reality, I can minister to only a few kids and adults at a time. I enjoyed the pats on the back, but I was failing at the kind of ministry I really wanted to do. It was only when I learned how to paint the picture with others that I really began to see my ministry expand and grow in the way it should. The best advertisement for any product is a satisfied customer, and that's exactly what you get when you are intentional about painting the picture. This is why it's so important to begin sharing the vision and clearly painting the picture with those around you as soon as possible.

PICTURING RESULTS

When you practice painting the picture of ministry, you will reap positive results. I saw the truth of this when I came to Long Hollow and there were about twenty-five workers in place in the student ministry. We all met together at a house and began to dream about what God could do through us and through Long Hollow. I painted a picture with them of what it would look like to have 500 students in our student ministry. At that time the church as a whole had between 800 and 1,000 people attending, so that picture was quite a stretch. But goals are supposed to stretch us when they are God's goals. I recognized that it was foundational for those core workers to develop a passion to reach students and to understand the plan we were going to use. That group of adults bought into the plan, and the picture we painted in a living room one day in March was a catalyst for unprecedented growth both spiritually and numerically.

Those workers and I first identified the need to expand from twenty-five to one hundred workers, and our goal was to do it by August. Of course, I was new to the area and had no clue who we could recruit. That's where painting the picture was so valuable. Because of the time we spent painting the picture and dreaming the dream, they knew who should be the next workers and who would best be able to come alongside in helping us reach the end goal. That's exactly what happened. By August we expanded to approximately one hundred workers, which prepared us for the students who were coming. As the new workers began to buy into the vision of the ministry, they began living out the picture that was painted in their own hearts. Thus they experienced life-change by understanding how they could be part of the work of God.

Other people began to see the difference in that group, and more and more people were noticing the excitement in student ministry. We celebrated the victories along the way, which will be explained more in chapter 5. The excitement became contagious, which encouraged others to get involved in the life-change themselves. People grew more passionate about Christ by seeing life-change and by celebrating the victories. Because the ministry revolved around more than just my personal efforts, it grew. Not necessarily because we marketed it well but because as a team, we painted a picture, involving others who became satisfied customers. We shared the vision in such a way that people lived out the plan in their hearts. When this happens, ministry becomes more than a program. It becomes a movement that spreads and grows.

For the movement to really take root in your ministry, the people involved — workers, parents, students — must begin to not just live it out but to paint the picture for others. The cool thing is that when they take ownership, whether as an adult or student, their life-change will be evident, and they'll be excited to share the vision and end goal with new people who can become involved too.

Understand that you don't just paint the picture for your adults and students, but for everyone. You share it wherever you go and with everyone you can—with school administrators, staff, coaches, parents. The goal is for everyone to see and understand what your vision is and what you're doing. I like to think about it this way: If I describe to a group of people what I'm craving at the moment by talking about a thick, moist yellow cake with chocolate icing, going into details about the height of the cake and the sweetness of the chocolate, then those listening can practically taste it for themselves. That's exactly the concept I'm using when I'm talking about the ministry plan and picture. My goal is to share it in such a way that those listening can "taste" it for themselves and be filled with the desire to be a part of it. I want them to be craving the life-change as much as I do, because then they will be willing to do whatever it takes to see it happen.

BURNING PASSION

If we get really good at communicating the plan and painting the picture for others, they will develop a burning passion to be part of something bigger than they are. After the Crucifixion and Resurrection, Jesus was walking with two of His followers along the Emmaus road. They didn't even recognize Him at first. Later, when they broke bread together, their eyes were opened and the men finally recognized Jesus (see Luke 24:13-35).

Jesus, in essence, painted a picture for them of their relationship, and the disciples went out from there and changed the world. So if our goal is to emulate Jesus by painting a picture, we must do it in such a way that people recognize Jesus for who He is and what He wants to do in and through them, to the point that they go out and change the world. When the disciples discussed what had happened, they referred to their "hearts burning within" (TNIV) them while Jesus talked to them on the road. I think they got the message, saw the picture, and understood the goal. That kind of motivation is irresistible. Our world is in desperate need of some student ministries that have a passion for life-change and are all about Jesus.

KEEP THE PICTURE FRESH

In the book of Leviticus, the priests are instructed to keep the wood on the altar burning and not let it go out. Once the passion starts burning in the hearts of people in the ministry, we must keep feeding the fire. Just as the priests had to put wood on the altar fire daily, we have to keep refreshing our picture to make sure that it doesn't get stale.

Have you ever pulled up a familiar website and noticed that it wasn't current? Our computers are trained to save images of sites, sort of like an unofficial bookmark, and it will open that old picture up instead of a current one sometimes until we refresh the page. The problem is that the old, saved picture isn't in real time and is out of date. The same thing can happen when we aren't refreshing ourselves, and thus our picture of ministry, regularly.

If God is always at work—and He is—then our picture may need tweaking along the way so that the information is current and up to date. If we aren't in the habit of refreshing our picture or plan for achieving our purpose, then the people around us, even within our ministry, may get frustrated because they really want to know what God is doing in the present. Today is extremely important, and we must not get trapped in the past to the point that our picture is out of date. Although there is value in reflecting on the past, which we will discuss fully in chapter 5, an important key to enduring, effective ministry is to keep your picture fresh and not let it get stale.

MAKE IT LAST

Is that your heart burning inside of you? I hope so. Do something about it. Let others see your passion and help them to start the fire inside of themselves as well. Use the questions in this section to paint the picture for your ministry plan.

1. What picture is in your heart and guiding your ministry right now? In previous chapters we discussed how the plan you develop helps you achieve your ministry's purpose. How does the picture you're painting now help you follow that plan?

2. How are you being intentional about painting a picture for the people in your ministry and on your team?

3. Have you effectively painted the picture for your church's executive pastor? If not, make a plan for how and when you will.

4. How are you allowing others to contribute their perspectives to the picture? If you're not doing this, come up with a way you can welcome and incorporate contributions from other people.

5. What are you doing to keep your picture fresh?

CHAPTER 4

MULTIPLY YOURSELF

Which do you like better, your foot or your hand? Which is more important, your ear or your eye? It sounds crazy to ask those kinds of questions, but they are the same types of comparisons that people are tempted to make in our ministries. Which position of service or leadership is more important than the others? This is not productive thinking, and we need to help everyone understand how valuable each person is to the work that God is doing.

Just as Paul wrote about the value of each body part in 1 Corinthians 12, it's important for us to realize the value in allowing each part of the body to work at its maximum level. Paul explained that the body is not made up of just one part, but many parts—the same is true of your life in ministry. It can't be just about you, the one student pastor. In order for ministry to be effective, you have to learn to multiply yourself. In doing this, you will enable the people in your ministry to contribute to God's work. When this happens, they will begin to see themselves as ministers also.

NOT ME BUT WE

It may sound funny to say, "I'm not the student pastor here," but I have realized that if I can get people to recognize that ministry is about a team mentality, then they will more fully engage in and buy into the ministry as a whole. I mentioned this in the first chapter, and now we can get into it a little more fully. Why? It works.

When I first came to Long Hollow, we had a meeting with lots of parents and staff, and I said these very words to the crowd: "I'm not the student minister here at Long Hollow." I paused. A voice from the crowd said, "If you aren't the student pastor here, then why did we hire you?" I responded with the rest of my statement: "We are." I shared with the group that this ministry wasn't going to be all about me. I told them I had some strengths but also many weaknesses, and I was going to need a lot of people around me contributing what only they can contribute in order for this ministry to be all that God wants it to be and in order for us to reach the students in our area with the gospel of Christ. It resonated with the group, and over time they began to see that *we* are the ministers, which is what Jesus described when He commanded us to go into the world and tell everyone the good news (see Mark 16:15). That verse is for all of us, not just those who are labeled as "pastor."

Too often in student ministry, pride becomes the driving force behind the leader or pastor. We want to prove our worth and make people see us as valuable in whatever capacity possible. When we become self-centered and self-focused, then the ministry becomes all about us. The goal is not to bring glory to ourselves but to equip the saints for the work of the Kingdom. I have learned that if I start with the adults and build a team that isn't based on me, I can reach more students and broaden the work of the student ministry. In essence, we as leaders must multiply ourselves so that the work of the ministry can be dramatically increased.

The truth is that our ministry can't be just about equipping students for the work of the Kingdom; it must help equip adults — staff, volunteers, and parents — too. When we realize the crucial role each group of people can play in our ministry, it will grow and endure. We must be intentional about our relationships with adults, whether workers or parents, and connect them to the part that God has for them in the work of this ministry. It's not as easy as working with the students, but it is vital. Workers need to see that ministry can't happen without them, and parents need to know and be reminded that they are still the most influential people in their students' lives.

Many parents miss this because they have adopted the mindset that if they drop their students off at church, the staff can take over and be whatever they need. Instead, we need to help our parents see that we want to partner with and come alongside them in raising their teens, and we desperately need them to be involved in the process. It's our job to equip parents with some tools that will be useful to them in discipling their own students. There are many things you can do along these lines.

At Long Hollow we offer parenting teenager classes and online helps for parents. We send out text messages to parents reminding them of important dates, hold parent meetings before camps and mission trips, and encourage parents to be involved in the ministry as a whole. We are always open to new ideas or ways we can better partner with the parents of our students. Anything you can do to involve parents will help them see that they have an important part in student ministry.

As you begin to multiply yourself, first by helping the youth workers, volunteers, and those on staff to recognize the importance of their involvement in the ministry, and second by involving students and parents, it will be important to get to know who you are working with. If you're new to your church, you will probably need to spend a significant amount of time just getting to know your team. Once you know who the other student ministers are, you can begin to strengthen, support, and grow them in their various areas of service.

RECOGNIZING STRENGTHS AND WEAKNESSES

At my first full-time church, I had a conversation with the pastor, Danny Wood. He said some things that have really stuck with me over the years. I shared about how I was working on many different things to improve myself and to grow and mature as a pastor. He challenged me to build on my strengths and stop focusing so much on my weaknesses.

Danny pointed out that the things I'm not as good at, like office paperwork and other clerical duties, are the definite strengths of other people. He wanted me to build my people skills and learn to develop my strengths for the glory of God and the work of the ministry. There were other people who thrived by working at a desk, but that wasn't me. That conversation changed my life and my ministry.

Think about it like this: If the eye is in charge of seeing and the ear is in charge of hearing, they have to recognize the valuable contributions they both make to the overall success of the body. The same is true of your ministry team, whether it's a paid staff team or a team of volunteers. You probably have people who feel like the most important thing to focus on is discipleship and meeting one-on-one with students. Some may believe it to be evangelism, others will want to focus on the details of ministry first, and still others will want it to be all about missions. The truth is that each one of those areas of focus is critical to your ministry just as each part of your body is vital in making the body function effectively.

The key for you as the pastor is to recognize the different strengths and weaknesses of your team so that each person can be serving in their "zone." The zone is that place where their giftedness matches up with the opportunities of ministry. You see the zone when Tiger Woods swings his club, Michael Jordan shoots the ball, or Peyton Manning throws a pass and the action seems so effortless. How can it seem so easy yet be so difficult to do well? Because they are operating in their zones. Their giftedness and abilities shine when they are using them to their full potential. The same thing happens when we steer people to serve in the way that God uniquely created them to serve. When they have the opportunity to connect their talents and interests with the needs of ministry, good things begin to happen.

You may be wondering how to recognize the skills and abilities of your people so that each is serving where they are most effective. How to help them get into their spiritual zone might sound like a big task. There are many resources available online that can help you with this discovery process. Spiritual gifts assessments and aptitude tests can be very helpful. Have your team take an assessment and evaluate the results with each team member individually. Depending upon the size of your team, you might review the results of only your leaders, and they can review the results of those they lead (other youth workers, volunteers, and students). As you encourage your leadership to discover their giftedness, you can then challenge your students to do the same.

When the people in your ministry recognize their unique gifts and abilities and are provided with opportunities to serve in those areas, good things will happen. They'll love serving because it meets a basic need in their life. Serving this way will also connect them with the purpose and the plan of ministry that will strengthen the principles you are working on. It all works together. This concept ties back to the main purpose of our ministry: to equip the saints to do the work of the ministry. God is pleased when He sees His children working in their zones, and your team of leaders and students will be excited and passionate about it too.

MOTIVATE, MOTIVATE, MOTIVATE

As you continue to get to know your team and see the unique qualities of each person, you will notice that they are also motivated in different ways. We tend to think that one motivation style will work for everyone, and we typically use the one that motivates us the best. Our body parts respond to specific stimuli, and so will your team. If you know your team, then you will be able to discover other ways to motivate and inspire them, increasing your ministry's effectiveness and building team unity.

As a male student pastor who grew up on athletic fields, I fell into the trap of attempting to motivate everyone around me in the way I had been motivated by coaches in the past. The problem was that

I worked around more women than men and my "coach" mentality wasn't computing with them. I had to find other ways to reach my target audience (the women working with me in ministry) in order to help them see the purpose, understand the plan, and see their role in the ministry as a whole.

Finding out what works best to motivate your team won't always be easy but you will find it worthwhile. I have discovered that I can learn a lot about motivation and learning styles when I surround myself with people whose talents and motivational styles are different from my own. Don't be afraid to ask for help and honest feedback. When it seems like you are not getting through to a certain group of people, ask questions that will give you insights into how that group thinks and reacts. Asking things like "If you had a completely free day, what would you plan to do?" "If you have a student in your small group who continually disrupts and draws attention away from you, what would you do?" or "What is the best way you can think of to encourage students?" will give you a better glimpse into those workers. As you get to know the people in your ministry, your own style will grow and broaden as well.

LEADERSHIP = LISTENING

Once you have people serving within their zones, it's important for them to be heard instead of the leader doing all of the talking. Good leadership recognizes that when people are working in their zones, they may very well know more about that aspect of the ministry than the leader does. I've come to recognize that once a person is in their zone, they don't really need me to come along and tell them every detail of how to do things and what to do next. At the same time, I've also learned in ministry that just helping people find their zone isn't quite enough. If people are serving in their ministry zone, we need to work with them, support them, and listen to their ideas of how things should happen because they are serving in a place that utilizes their strengths. It's delegation at its best and will lead team members to grow and develop into the people God created them to be as they strengthen the body as a whole.

It's imperative for every person involved in your ministry to see his or her role as vital. If they do, you'll find that you don't have to remind them to be at church or youth services. They will be there because they know they are important to the ministry. You won't have to badger students and volunteers to sign up for camp or other events because they'll already know they have an important part to play.

To use another athletic analogy, this is much like football. A football coach needs to see every person on the team as crucial to the success of the team. If the center doesn't get the ball into the quarterback's hands, the play will fail. If the guard doesn't block, then someone will hit the ground. And if the equipment manager doesn't outfit the players in the correct gear, the whole team is in trouble. Although the quarterback may get the most press, without the equipment manager the game could not happen correctly. It's the job of the coach to see the importance of each team member and to help team members realize that he sees them as crucial to the success of the team.

The same is true for the student pastor. If you want the people surrounding you to see themselves as important to the ministry, it's critical that you value the role of every volunteer and student, recognizing their importance to the ministry's overall success. Whether they are taking roll, greeting people by name, teaching a lesson, bringing snacks, or making contacts during the week, each person has a role to fill, and your job is to let them know that you couldn't do ministry without them. I always tell my team of volunteers not only that I can't do ministry without them but also that I refuse to do ministry without them.

LEAD BY EXAMPLE

As we accomplish our goal of involving people in the ministry, we have to remember never to ask them to do what we ourselves aren't willing to do. We should be willing to go the extra mile and lead in everything. Delegation is not relegation. We might delegate a task to someone, but it's still our responsibility to make sure the task is being completed and that what we're doing fits with our purpose and plan.

At the end of the day, we're still the staff person in charge. People need to see us doing things we don't even like to do, that we're maybe not even good at, because seeing us try means more to our team members than we can know. As you think about this, you might realize that you need to stay visible. If there are workers serving in their zones, which aren't necessarily your own areas of strength, it's valuable to ask them what you can do to help out. This reinforces the idea that we're all on the same team.

A student pastor I highly respect once told me that it never hurts to be the first one there and the last one to leave. Ministry is hard work. When it comes down to it, you and I as student pastors need to be working the hardest and setting the pace. Too many times, and with good reason, pastors are labeled as lazy. It's up to us to be seen as one who works hard and does it in honor of the Lord.

EQUIP AND TRAIN

If we want people involved in the ministry and serving in their giftedness, we must take seriously our instruction to equip and train. People don't like to be part of an organization if they don't feel equipped to do their job. Many times the reason others don't want to get involved is because they feel unprepared. When prospective workers realize that you're going to walk with them and train them along the way, they will be even more willing to serve and work.

Our goal as student ministers is to have satisfied customers in our students, parents, and adult workers. When people serve in their zones and receive the necessary training and equipping, they become the most excited and passionate advertisements for the ministry. Satisfied customers recruit others like themselves to be involved in what's going on. People will only feel frustration if we fail to equip and train them.

A basic model of equipping that I have used for years is this: huddle weekly, fellowship monthly, and train yearly. Understand that training takes place all year long and is ongoing, but once a year it's beneficial to have organized, large-group training events for all volunteers and workers.

A weekly huddle is all about connecting. This can be done in person, online, by text, or however best fits your ministry. The goal is the same as that of a huddle in a ball game: to get all of the team on the same page. We often do this just before the student small-group time on Sunday mornings. It doesn't need to last long but is perfect for touching base and talking over any details. Always take time to pray over your workers and then break the huddle so that the team can disperse and accomplish the goals of the day.

Monthly fellowship is all about gathering together and building team unity. You can have a dessert fellowship, potluck supper, or other type of gathering that builds community. Talk about what is happening in the ministry and celebrate the good things God is doing. You may address some upcoming events and even share new principles of leadership that will help your volunteers. This is totally focused on them feeling part of the body or team and knowing they are not alone.

With yearly corporate training for your adult leadership, you can paint the big picture of what will be happening in the coming months and share strategic ideas for the different aspects of the ministry—teaching, outreach, evangelism, and so forth. Workers should divide into groups of people currently serving within the same area of ministry so that they can learn from one another ways to do their jobs more effectively. Gather your workers by assignments. If you have small group, care group, outreach, or other types of leaders, they can do some peer learning as they discuss what works well for their particular responsibilities. It is also a great time for those leaders to share their struggles and seek insight from others who are working in the same area. You can also use this time for general motivation and challenge. You might consider enlisting a speaker — this can be someone from within or outside of your church — to address the entire group of student workers. You'll also want to talk about the year as a whole and highlight any special events or emphasis that may be coming soon. Another advantage for this time is that you can share a theme for the year to promote cohesiveness.

SETTING STANDARDS

Though our desire is for many people to be involved in the ministry, there needs to be certain qualifications for different levels of service. At Long Hollow if you want to work in the student ministry, you must fill out an application form. This covers not only personal information but also doctrinal beliefs, covenant requirements, and personal testimony. We also interview each person interested in working before they begin. This is to make sure they know our philosophy of student ministry, and it serves as a way for us to get to know them. Our goal is not just to fill a position but to fill a position with a person who is equipped for that role. Our students are valuable to us, and we won't trust them to just anyone.

For that reason, part of the interview process with new workers involves a background check. We want to protect our students mentally, spiritually, and physically. In today's world, we can't be too careful about who we allow to lead students. If you're worried about offending people, don't be. We have found that people with nothing to hide have no problem with these constraints and, in fact, appreciate that we are willing to protect our students. It is much better to find things out before a situation arises, and this procedure will help protect your students and the church as a whole.

We believe by raising the bar of what we expect from our workers, we see much greater results. If we set the bar too low, it creates a ceiling on what will be accomplished, but when that bar is raised, we are all continually striving to reach new heights. With God all things are possible, so let's be the ones who go for it. Multiply yourself. Multiply the ministry. Multiply the life-change.

MAKE IT LAST

It's possible you've felt overwhelmed before, trying to do everything in your ministry by yourself. Take a few minutes to reflect on the chapter as you answer these questions, and consider how multiplying yourself can improve the effectiveness of your ministry.

1. How are you multiplying yourself in your ministry? If you're not, make a plan for how you will delegate some responsibilities to others.

2. Would you say that your ministry is about you or about the team? If you were to ask one of the members of your ministry, what would they say?

3. Do you have a sense that you are doing everything? If so, how can you be more intentional about allowing others to take part?

4. What is your strategy for equipping? Does it encompass all three groups of people (students, workers, and parents)?

5. In what ways (if any) have you set a low ceiling for your ministry?

CHAPTER 5

CELEBRATE EARLY AND OFTEN

Everybody likes a party. Even the people who say they don't are probably just protecting themselves from the disappointment that may come if they aren't invited. Parties are all about celebrating. Birthdays. Anniversaries. Weddings. Babies. A party can be about celebrating almost anything.

Actually, celebration was dictated and ordained by God in the Old Testament when He instructed the Israelites to celebrate every year with seven feasts. These were each specifically designed to remind the people who God was and what He had done in their lives. They were supposed to celebrate and party about their God. Sound familiar? We need to be doing the same thing.

In the church today we have the greatest reason ever to celebrate: life-change. Yet too often we get busy with the work of ministry and overlook the call to celebrate. The next principle of building an effective ministry is to celebrate early and often. In this chapter we will break down the reasons we need to celebrate and also some practical ways to be intentional about celebrating. If it was important to the Lord, it should be important to us.

A PARTY WAITING TO HAPPEN

Have you ever met a person who by his personality was a party waiting to happen? When I think about celebrating and those types of people, I think about Jesus. People went out of their way to get to Him. Men were so desperate to get in on what was happening with Jesus that they cut through a roof and lowered their buddy into the house. Others went out of their way, hiked miles upon miles, just to bring blind and lame people to see Him. Why? Because Jesus was all about life-change, and He didn't hesitate to celebrate that life-change with those around Him.

I always remind my students and team to celebrate early and often. It's impossible to make too big of a deal about life-change. God commanded people to celebrate it. Jesus set a great example of it. We must be intentional about it.

In churches and student ministry in particular, we need to be sure we are focused on life-change. It's our responsibility to "whoop it up" about the work we see the Holy Spirit doing in the lives of those in our ministries. When we create an atmosphere that is ready to celebrate life-change at the drop of a hat, people will be drawn to our ministries just as Jesus drew people.

For me this started back at my first church with a youth group of about twenty people. We had our Wednesday night youth service, and a couple of students brought friends who accepted Christ. We purposely made a big deal out of both the students who accepted Christ and the ones who brought them. It's important to celebrate those who brought their friends so that others want to do the same thing.

We also celebrated the life-change of the lost friends who were brought to church and asked Jesus into their hearts. The fact that those friends had become new creations in Christ was reason to party. This intentional celebrating encourages the new believers and opens the eyes of people to see that God is at work and changing lives. Celebrating both the new believers and the friends who introduced them to Christ is powerful. When we apply this principle to our ministries, it will be contagious, and knowing Christ will become more attractive to the students around us. In essence, everybody will want to get in on the party.

CONTAGIOUS CELEBRATION

Our goal is that a movement of God starts and continues to grow as we are intentional about working the plan, with the picture painted for all to see. The things that we've been discussing in the previous chapters are all coming together as we learn to celebrate the things that only God can do.

If you really understand who Jesus is and the fact that He is alive and working in and through you, then you should be ready to celebrate and get in on the party. The truth is that people are attracted to excitement, fun, and unique experiences. Jesus was a magnet; He was unlike anyone else. He drew people to Himself and He continues to do so in our world today. When God starts working and doing things that only He can do, people become excited and want to be involved; it's contagious. Contagious is good when what's happening is 100 percent God's doing. I always want to be serving in a place where I can't explain what's happening except to say, "It must be God."

Consider what happened when Jesus encountered the Samaritan woman in John 4. He spoke with her, and her life was changed. In her excitement, she rushed back to town and told everyone about her experience. It intrigued the townspeople to see the change in her, and they were drawn to experience it for themselves. The woman invited the people to come and meet Jesus and then led them back to Him. Think about what a party they had at the well that day.

Scripture tells us that many of the townspeople believed in Jesus and even invited Him to stay for a few days. Do you see it? One woman's experience with Jesus started a movement that changed a town! That's exactly what we want to see in our student ministries. Not only did many people believe, but they told the woman that they believed for themselves and not just because of what she said. These people began to own their faith because of their personal experiences with Christ. As we discussed in chapter 2, we must be intentional about equipping our students to own their faith, because as they do and as we celebrate it, others will be excited to join God and us in fulfilling the purpose of our ministry.

CELEBRATE THE PAST AND THE PRESENT

Our celebration needs to follow the example of the children of Israel. They continually told the stories of the great and mighty things God had done for them and their families. The reasoning was twofold: so that they didn't forget and so that those who weren't present could celebrate along with them.

In student ministry we need to tell the stories of where God has led us and what He has brought us through. We can rejoice over the fact that God has done great and mighty things through our ministries. For instance, during a meeting with our church's resource team (the people who handle finances, personnel, and all other resources), I started my portion of the meeting by recounting with them all the life-change we had seen during the past year. I reminded them of the number of students we baptized, the number involved in small groups, and the number of those who had professed Jesus as Savior. This served to encourage them not only about what we have done in student ministry but also about what we can do in the future. Celebrating the past is vital to strengthening our faith for the future, but we can't stop there.

There is a temptation to hang out in the glory days of the past and get stuck there. While celebrating past successes is important, remember that the journey is not complete. The God of the past is the God of today and tomorrow, so we also need to be talking about and celebrating the things that He is up to right now. We make it a point to share life-change stories with our church as a whole through testimonies, either by video or in person. We sometimes hold special baptism services at a lake, pool, or portable baptistery in the parking lot. There is no end to the ways that you can celebrate, and whether it is by inviting the congregation to clap, sing, or yell and shout, the point is that you celebrate. Whatever that looks like in your church is what you should do.

Being intentional about inviting people to celebrate with you will yield great reward. In student ministry, you always want to see new people getting involved. When you make a habit of telling the stories and celebrating from the past to the present, they get to see all God has done and is doing. This leads to a stronger sense of belonging and confidence in the ministry and builds excitement in general.

The Bible says to "rejoice with those who rejoice" (Romans 12:15, TNIV), and we take that seriously. After nine years at one church, it's amazing to see the number of people who can tell the stories for me. It really doesn't get old. It's kind of like those stories your parents tell about when you were little that make you smile because you know you play a major role in the plot.

When I tell the story of where our ministry started and all that God has done, student after student begins to smile and nod because they recognize that it's about them. They have a role in the story, and God is still using them as He continues to write it. The newer students begin to look for ways to get involved in the story so that the next time we are celebrating the work of God, they are in the story too. These are powerful times and should never be overlooked.

CELEBRATION WORTH STOPPING FOR

A program-driven ministry moves from one calendar event to the next, many times so quickly that celebration is lost in the shuffle. We can't let this happen. Ministry is not just about the program but about life-change. This doesn't negate the validity of programming and calendaring. Ministry is too important to just fly by the seat of your pants. But it is also too important to be just another checklist you complete to feel better about yourself. We need to plan, organize, and schedule; however, we need to be intentional about retaining time to celebrate.

Have you gotten in the habit of moving from one thing to the next without celebrating God's successes and accomplishments? It's easy to be so performance based and production oriented that we go from one event to the next. Many student pastors, like myself, struggle with being performance-driven people. My natural bent is to prove my self-worth by how much I get done. The easiest way to do that is to plan out and pull off event after event or program after program. The reality is that if I truly want to reach people with the gospel, then I am going to do that most effectively when I lay aside my natural self and follow the plan and example of Jesus, to do everything as unto the Lord and only what my Father has commanded me. It's not about works; it's about obedience.

If you face some of the same struggles of being performance driven, then it's important to be transparent with your students and team. I try to be intentional about stressing that this ministry is not about me but about all of us working together, just as we talked about in chapter 4. People in your ministry want to see a pastor who doesn't have all the answers but who is a work in progress and celebrates God's power in his life. They can relate to that person and will be more open to connecting with the Savior you are talking about.

Make sure that as you plan your year and schedule your days, you find times to reflect on the work of God in your life and ministry. Celebration is worth stopping for because it creates momentum, and movements are fueled by momentum.

CELEBRATION IS MOTIVATION

Celebration creates momentum because it motivates the people involved. They are attracted to God's activity in people's lives, not to the program. I don't mean to minimize the value of certain events or programs that draw people, because we can certainly see the truth of that. But we do all these events and programs for a reason. As we talked about in chapter 1, it goes back to purpose. The program may attract their attention, but it's the activity of God and the life-change they see and experience that will draw them to continue attending and serving.

Think about it this way: The plan, program, and calendar tend to point people to the pastor and shine the light on your effort. Our goal should be to point people to Christ and the life-change He brings. That's the role of celebrating, so that the plan, program, and calendar can shine the light on the Light of the World.

CELEBRATE INDIVIDUALS

Our focus so far has been on the why of celebrating, and I've shared examples of corporate celebrating through planned services, testimonies, and telling stories. As a student pastor, you also need to be intentional about celebrating with the individuals of your ministry. This needs to be about your students, your volunteers, and your parents.

A great example of celebrating on the individual level is with a set of twin boys who grew up in an unchurched family in our community. They were invited to camp by friends from school, and both boys came to know Christ at camp. At our Camp Celebration Service back home, with a room full of parents and friends, Jason and Justin were baptized.

From there we built relationships with the twins, and they became more and more involved in the student ministry. Both boys started reaching out to their friends and sharing Christ with others. Today we can't count the number of people who have been saved as a result of those boys' life-change. We stayed with them along the journey and kept making a big deal by celebrating what God was doing in and through them, from the small life-change to the more dramatic. It hasn't been easy for them to live godly lives with so many unsaved people in their family, and they haven't always done it perfectly, but Jason and Justin have learned to stay faithful and be obedient.

Celebrating with the twins has helped to build confidence in them and their personal relationships with the Lord. It has empowered them to boldly share the gospel with those around them. If we learn to make a big deal with students as they experience life-change, it will fuel their enthusiasm to continue doing what God wants them to do. That will lead to even more spiritual growth.

While celebrating with your students is important, celebrating with your workers is also critical to an effective ministry. So how do you celebrate with your adult volunteers, and why is it so important? You may know someone like Mike. Mike was a high school baseball coach who didn't think he was equipped to work with students at church. He felt like he didn't have anything to give them spiritually. Although he was a Christian and worked with guys every day on the baseball field, spiritually speaking he felt deficient.

I built a relationship with Mike and began talking to him about serving on our volunteer team. He was resistant at first but then decided to give it a try. During that first year, I checked on Mike a lot to see how he was doing and offered any support and coaching he might need. There were some difficult times as he led that group of boys when he didn't feel like they were connecting with his lessons or they became irregular attendees. The good news is that there were also some good times when he saw the guys engage with the Word of God and start to live differently because of it, acting in a more godly manner at school.

Both the good and the challenging were times of celebration with Mike. We celebrated everything from having a good group discussion to persevering through difficulties. The key is that we celebrated. At the end of that year, we reflected on all he had learned and how God had used him.

Six years later, Mike is still working with students. He has grown personally through serving these students. His family has also been impacted and is involved in the ministry with him. The relationships he has with the students he has poured himself into are priceless. If we hadn't taken the time to celebrate along the way with Mike, he might have given up and stepped back. Our ministry would have missed him, and most importantly he would have missed out on how God wanted to use him.

It's not just volunteers who need encouragement, though. Remember when we talked about the importance of involving parents in your ministry? Well, parents need to be celebrated too! One of my favorite parent examples happened with Larry. He had a son in our student ministry named Judson. I began to develop a relationship with Larry, who at the time was involved in the church but didn't necessarily see the correlation between his church experience and Judson's. Over the course of time he began to realize just how much they were connected.

As Judson became more and more involved in the ministry, Larry and his wife became increasingly involved as well. It all goes back to chapter 4 and recognizing that everyone has a role to fill. I celebrated with Larry about what was happening in Judson's life and in their relationship. I made a big deal about how he and his wife were being used in their son's spiritual development. This helped Larry to grow spiritually and Judson to mature into the man God called him to be.

Our churches are full of parents who might understand to a certain degree what it means for their students to be involved in student ministry. When we learn to celebrate with those parents, they will be more aware of how much God is doing in the students' lives. They will want to be more involved, and that's what we need. We want parents to get involved in discipling their children.

We at the church are only able to spend a few hours a week with the students (if we're lucky!). The more we are able to equip and excite parents about leading their students spiritually, the more the ministry will grow. The more the parents get involved, the more they become your biggest support, and they will rally other parents to do the same. Parents who understand this concept of leading their students spiritually will bring other parents along to do the same. This is awesome, and it happens when we have celebrated personal growth and student life-change with parents all along the way.

INITIATING CELEBRATION

You might find as you begin celebrating with individuals in your ministry that you're the only one initiating these times of encouragement. That's okay. But as your ministry grows, it will become important for you to train your workers to do the celebrating too. This will broaden the scope of the celebrations, and more people will become involved. Small groups are the most natural place for the individual celebrating with students to occur. If you have two adult workers with ten or so students, they will be able to do the ministry of celebrating in a manageable way.

Keeping up with the adult volunteers will depend on the number that you have. As our ministry has grown at Long Hollow, we have created roles for some volunteers to be the care group ministers for the other adult workers. These people contact and keep in touch with the individual workers and let the pastors know when significant life-change is happening and needs to be celebrated. Once again, by sharing the load, more people get involved in what God is doing, and the ministry is multiplied.

CELEBRATE CREATIVELY

We're all creative. The God of the universe created us in His image and He is the ultimate Creator. That means we can't use the excuse of not being creative to limit the celebration that happens. We need to get creative in the ways we celebrate life-change. If we are willing to make a creative video as a promotion for an event or develop a website that grabs attention, we should be willing to expend some effort into creative celebration.

One key is to get a lot of involvement in the planning process. Invite others to share in developing a plan of how you can better celebrate creatively with your students, workers, and parents. Whether it's having a celebration baptism service, creative video testimonies, or an old-school handwritten note of encouragement, there is power in celebration. I have discovered that students like videos they can laugh and engage with, but a handwritten card or note that celebrates what God has done will be saved and reread over and over. It may be a lost art to send cards and notes, but we can bring it back and revitalize it for our ministries. The tool is not the most important thing, the celebration is.

Baptism is one of the most visual displays of life-change, so you also need to think about creative ways of involving family and friends with baptisms. You can provide personalized videos of the student's baptism for the family. One year we baptized students in a swimming pool, and those who supported and encouraged the students stood in the pool with them. We've done similar things when we performed baptisms at the lake. When we've used a portable baptistery, we invited the family and friends to gather around the baptistery in support. It creates a meaningful experience and enlarges the celebration.

We always make a big deal out of baptism and encourage others to as well. It is not unusual to hear cheering and clapping when students go through the baptismal waters—even if it's during a Sunday morning service. We like to challenge others' perceptions of our exuberance over life-change with how excited people get at a ball game. I often make comparisons between excitement over athletics and how baptism is a picture of the ultimate life-change with eternal rewards. Let's face it, if we get super excited when our team scores a goal, then how can we not get excited when someone's life is changed for eternity?

There is no end to the ways that you can celebrate what God is doing because there is no end to what He is doing. We have to recognize that God is continually at work all around us, and that, my friend, is cause for celebration! Throw a party; they will come.

MAKE IT LAST

Use the questions in this section to evaluate how celebration could or already does impact your ministry.

1. List three things that you are specifically (and intentionally) doing to celebrate life-change in your ministry.

2. What is the most creative celebration you can think of?

3. How are you celebrating individually with students, parents, and workers?

4. Have you been intentional about training your workers to celebrate? If not, then what will you do differently?

5. Have you become so program driven that you don't take time to stop and celebrate? If so, what will you change to make celebrating a priority?

CHAPTER 6

POWER FOR CHANGE

There's one final thought I want to leave you with. It's true, understanding your ministry's purpose, developing the plan, painting the picture, multiplying yourself, and celebrating life-change are all foundational principles of building an effective student ministry that will endure, but we must recognize that it's only by the power of Christ that anything is accomplished. One of my favorite verses is Philippians 4:13. In ministry we need to realize that we can do all things through Christ who strengthens us, but only He can give us the strength we need.

One summer when I was the student pastor at a church in Florida, we were at youth camp. During one of the services I was seated beside the senior pastor, and I kept feeling like something needed to be done during the service. I mentioned the feeling to him, and he spoke some strong words in return that still impact me today. He said, "The last time I looked, you were the pastor of this student ministry. If you feel like something needs to happen, then you are responsible for responding to what God is saying to you." I realized then that I wasn't just a pastor in charge of programming and planning; most importantly, I was responsible for the spiritual well-being of the students in the ministry. When I feel God leading me in a direction, I need to respond.

Because you and I are the spiritual leaders of our ministries, it is vitally important that we stay connected and "charged up" spiritually. This means we are to continually be fed and refreshed by the power of the Holy Spirit in our lives. The old saying that you can't lead someone farther than you have gone is even more true for us spiritually.

There have been many times in ministry when I've found myself substituting preparation for a Wednesday night sermon or Sunday morning Bible study in place of my personal quiet time. This is unacceptable. We must take time to be alone with the Lord or we will become spiritually dry. This will affect not only us but also those in our ministry. I have heard it said this way: "Never substitute public ministry for private devotion."

ACCOUNTABILITY IS CRUCIAL

As a student pastor, your spiritual health must be a priority. Just as there are many factors that affect your physical health, there are also many factors to consider in strengthening your spiritual health. Accountability is a valuable contributor that sometimes is overlooked. It may be because many times we make decisions on our own. Yes, we may have the right to make decisions, but we will be better pastors if we have people in our lives to keep us accountable for our actions and spiritual development.

Accountability helps us prepare for the battles that will come our way. It's great to lead a student ministry that is effective, but as a student ministry grows, there will be spiritual warfare. The Enemy isn't happy when students reconcile with the Lord, and he will do all he can to stop it. There can be a tendency in ministry leadership to isolate ourselves, but that creates dangerous situations the Enemy is eager to take advantage of. We set ourselves up for attack and failure when we choose to minister without having someone in our lives who cares for us enough to ask the hard questions about our spiritual health. Isolation is for contagious diseases not Christians.

Another form of accountability that strengthens our spiritual health is found through small groups. We need to be involved in a small group of adults with whom we can do life together as well as study the Bible. Understand that your small-group interaction will probably need to take place sometime other than a Sunday morning, since when we are at church we are working. You may even have to organize a group like this yourself, but you will find it to be very rewarding and worth the effort.

I'll confess, I haven't always done this, but after twenty-nine years of ministry I can honestly say that one thing I wish I had made a priority everywhere I served was being in a small group with my wife. The benefits of discussing how Scripture applies to my life, as well as just spending time with other people who are doing life in the same stage as me, has been one of the most effective accountability tools.

One of the most intentional and sometimes difficult parts of accountability is having a few men (if you're a male) or women (if you're a woman) whom you can go to for straight answers. These need to be people you have given permission to ask you the hard questions and get in your face when you need to be challenged about something. You don't want them to be people who will say what you *want* to hear, but people who will say what you *need* to hear. There is much wisdom in godly counsel, and this is crucial if you want to lead well.

One of the most godly and wise Christian leaders in the world is Billy Graham. I had the privilege of being part of the leadership team for one of his crusades. The crusade was a powerful time, and I believe that the key to that power is prayer. The Graham Crusade team constantly challenged any and all people helping with the crusade to pray.

I watched the way they prayed over the crusade and noticed that it raised the spiritual temperature of the event as a whole. What I learned is that if you want to see the power of God in your ministry, you need to pray. First you need to pray for yourself as the pastor. Next you need to pray for the people who are involved in your ministry or who need to be involved. Third, you need to pray about whatever it is that you're attempting to do, whether it's an event, camp, or ongoing activities. By praying, especially when praying with others, you can encourage each other to continue to uphold what God has spoken to you.

FROM THE INSIDE OUT

A discussion about the power of God in your ministry starts with you as the leader and then radiates out to the people in your ministry. First you need to be where God wants you to be spiritually, then you need to allow His power to work through you, setting you free from your own limitations. Consider yourself a spiritual thermostat. That means it's your responsibility to set the spiritual temperature in your ministry. When others see your spiritual life thriving as you allow God to be the Lord of everything you do, they will want to allow His power to work through them too.

Setting the temperature is tied up with expectations. Don't under-challenge people spiritually. Whether they're serving or participating in Bible study, worship, or mission work, in every way possible raise the bar for people spiritually. This goes back to your vision and your picture of how ministry needs to happen. One aspect of your picture that you want to focus on is what you expect to see God do spiritually. Never underestimate God's power, and always challenge students and others in your ministry to take risks and trust Him. Remember, low expectations will inevitably be met. When you start raising the bar, you will begin to see the power of God at work. He is more than capable of blowing our minds spiritually.

What are you doing to raise the spiritual expectations for your student ministry? We need to think about this question practically and intentionally. Do you want them to pray more, know the Bible better, be more mission minded, love Jesus more? The answer to all these questions is "yes." If you agree, then you need to evaluate what you're doing to make it a reality.

Could it be possible that we in ministry have bought into the mentality of today's culture that says everyone gets a trophy for just showing up? By doing that, we are lowering our expectations of the power of God at work in our lives. God is bigger than that. Our students deserve to reach for the prize or go for the goal, and it's our job to give them that opportunity. This happens when we raise the bar.

There is nothing as gratifying as seeing students really grasp this concept and develop a hunger and thirst for God. Nothing can compare to leading students who have a passion burning within them to live differently and make a difference in this world. Student ministries across the country bemoan the numbers of students who leave the church when they leave high school. Fortunately I have seen the opposite to be true.

It overwhelms me to consider the number of students I've worked with who have found their calling in ministry. That's the power of God. When I am blessed to serve on staff at churches alongside former students, I see the power of God at work. When I hear from college students who graduated from our ministry and are now starting their own mission efforts or are feeding the homeless, I see the power of God. When I talk to young adults who came through our student ministry and are now married and raising kids who love Jesus, that's even more evidence of the power of God.

What we do by leading in student ministry is a big deal. It is much bigger than anything of this earth because the results are eternal and, truthfully, it's hard work. The days of sitting behind a desk in an office and waiting for students to show up is long gone. If we want to impact this generation with the gospel, then you and I have to "get after it." We have to go out into the real world and let people see and hear about the difference that Jesus makes. That, my friend, happens by the power of the Holy Spirit working in and through you. Believe it, and don't settle for less than that power.

As we work to equip the saints for ministry, may we never be guilty of limiting what God does because we didn't expect much. I firmly believe that when we practice raising the bar and setting our expectations high, we will see a generation of students rise to the challenge. They are waiting for something bigger than themselves to believe in and fight for. We can help them fight, and the victory is ours if we choose to live in the power of almighty God.

The challenge is before you.

It's time.

NOTES

1. The Fuller Institute, George Barna, Pastoral Care, Inc.,
   "Statistics: Why Pastors Leave the Ministry," Pastoral Care, Inc.,
   2009, http://pastoralcareinc.com/WhyPastoralCare/Statistics.php
   (accessed May 11, 2011).
2. Jim Collins, *Good to Great* (New York: HarperCollins, 2001), 1.

ABOUT THE AUTHOR

Jeff Lovingood is a longtime veteran of student ministry and is currently serving as next generation pastor at Long Hollow Church in Hendersonville, Tennessee. Although Jeff typically describes himself as "an old country youth pastor," plain-spoken and straightforward, he is a true practitioner who lives out his ministry philosophy in everyday life. Having served in churches of all sizes, he refined and developed the principles for developing an effective youth ministry from his practical work in the field. Through his work in the ministry, Jeff has had the privilege of helping thousands of students and adults experience life-change and find their place in ministry.

Having come to the realization at an early age that God was calling him to ministry, Jeff earned degrees at Carson Newman College and Southwestern Baptist Theological Seminary in preparation for future roles in ministry leadership.

Jeff loves to play any and every sport (except soccer) but values time with his family above all else. He is married to Rachel, an author, speaker, and mother of their three children: Trevor and Kelsey, who are college students, and Riley, who is in high school. As Jeff will tell you, raising kids while serving in ministry is both challenging and rewarding, but the lessons he has learned as a parent have helped shape and motivate his intentional ministry to parents as well as students.

MY LIFE IS **TOUGHER** THAN MOST **PEOPLE REALIZE.**

I TRY TO
KEEP EVERYTHING
IN BALANCE:
FRIENDS, FAMILY, WORK,
SCHOOL, AND GOD.

IT'S NOT EASY.

I KNOW WHAT MY
PARENTS BELIEVE AND
WHAT MY PASTOR SAYS.

BUT IT'S NOT
ABOUT THEM.
IT'S ABOUT ME...

ISN'T IT TIME I
OWN MY FAITH?

THROUGH THICK AND THIN, KEEP YOUR HEARTS AT ATTENTION, IN
ADORATION BEFORE CHRIST, YOUR MASTER. BE READY TO SPEAK
UP AND TELL ANYONE WHO ASKS WHY YOU'RE LIVING THE WAY
YOU ARE, AND ALWAYS WITH THE UTMOST COURTESY. 1 PETER 3:15 (MSG)

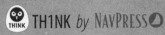

www.navpress.com | 1-800-366-7788